# In Praise of Ambivalence

# In Praise of Ambivalence

D. JUSTIN COATES

OXFORD
UNIVERSITY PRESS

## OXFORD
UNIVERSITY PRESS

Oxford University Press is a department of the University of Oxford. It furthers
the University's objective of excellence in research, scholarship, and education
by publishing worldwide. Oxford is a registered trade mark of Oxford University
Press in the UK and certain other countries.

Published in the United States of America by Oxford University Press
198 Madison Avenue, New York, NY 10016, United States of America.

Library of Congress Cataloging-in-Publication Data
Names: Coates, D. Justin, author.
Title: In praise of ambivalence / D. Justin Coates.
Description: New York, NY, United States of America : Oxford University Press, [2023] |
Includes bibliographical references and index.
Identifiers: LCCN 2022029982 (print) | LCCN 2022029983 (ebook) |
ISBN 9780197652398 (hardback) | ISBN 9780197652411 (epub)
Subjects: LCSH: Ambivalence.
Classification: LCC BF575.A45 C63 2023 (print) | LCC BF575.A45 (ebook) |
DDC 128/.4—dc23/eng/20220825
LC record available at https://lccn.loc.gov/2022029982
LC ebook record available at https://lccn.loc.gov/2022029983

DOI: 10.1093/oso/9780197652398.001.0001

1 3 5 7 9 8 6 4 2

Printed by Integrated Books International, United States of America

*Dedicated with Love*
To Stephanie, Pearl, and Irene

# Contents

# Acknowledgments

This main ideas in this book are ones I've been thinking through for nearly a decade. In that time, I've talked to dozens of people about them, and in almost every case, learned something important. It is doubtful that I will remember everyone who has had a hand in helping me develop and refine these ideas, but I am deeply grateful for the help all the same. This book would not exist without the significant support I've received from so many wonderful philosophers. Nor would it exist without the love of my wife Stephanie and our daughters, Pearl and Irene.

Versions of Chapters 3, 7, and 8 were presented at Georgia State University, Rice University, and the Texas Ethics Workshop at Texas Christian University, and I am appreciative of the feedback I received at these venues from Jessica Berry, Gwen Bradford, Amy Floweree, Alida Liberman, Eddy Nahmias, Tim O'Keefe, Jeremy Sakovich, Timothy Schroeder, and George Sher. I am also thankful to Sarah Buss, John Martin Fischer, Samantha Matherne, Neal Tognazzini, and two anonymous referees who commented on the paper "A Wholehearted Defense of Ambivalence," which overlaps significantly with parts of Chapters 2 and 3 of this book. So too, I appreciate the extremely helpful feedback I received from two anonymous referees and my editor, Peter Ohlin, for his help in shepherding the manuscript to completion.

Informal conversations with my colleagues Luis Oliveira, Tamler Sommers, David Phillips, and Helen Hattab have also informed and improved aspects of the book. I'm thankful for both these conversations and for the collegial atmosphere in our department. I am also grateful to the students in my Fall 2021 graduate seminar for reading and commenting on the book manuscript: Chance Bazz, Caroline Castigliola, Sze Hoi Chan, Paulina Ezquerra, Jake Green, Barrett Hess, Ariel Kaplan, Quentin Leblanc, Graham Lee, Regina Sainz, Rose Sanchez, Gretchen Schmaltz, and Jay Thomas. Sustained discussions with Ben Mitchell-Yellin, Christopher Franklin, Philip Swenson, Dave Beglin, and Andrew Eshleman have also helped me refine the arguments here. But most of all, I am especially grateful to Neal Tognazzini, Dan Speak, and Garrett Pendergraft, who read full drafts of this book at a relatively early stage. Their feedback and encouragement were invaluable for this book. I am lucky to have friends, students, and colleagues like these.

# 1

# Introduction

## 1.1. The Problem of Ambivalence

The experience of being ambivalent is familiar enough. When faced with a difficult decision, we often feel not just unsure of ourselves but divided or torn about what to do. This is particularly true when whatever we decide, we'll have to give up on something that we're deeply committed to, something that speaks to who we are as individuals. In fact, in these sorts of cases, it genuinely feels that however we ultimately choose, we'll be betraying ourselves in some important way.

These feelings often track something real. Consider Erica, for example, who finds herself with an exciting new job offer on the other side of the country. This opportunity, we can imagine, truly is the culmination of years of very hard work on her part. It's something she has wanted very badly for a long time and now it's within her grasp. Yet, if she accepts it, Erica won't be able to continue being close to her aging parents, for whom she is the primary caregiver. But her role as caregiver is also something that she deeply identifies with and values. It seems that in the particular scenario Erica finds herself in, she cannot choose in a way that does justice to each element of who she is: if she takes the job, then she'll have to give up her role as a caregiver for her parents, but if she refuses the job, then she'll no longer be able to regard her career ambitions, as well as all of the hard work she has done in pursuit of those goals in quite the same way. In other words, it will turn out that however she chooses, she will fail to honor some key aspect of who she is. It's only natural, then, that Erica finds herself anguished over the decision. Her

*In Praise of Ambivalence*. D. Justin Coates, Oxford University Press. © Oxford University Press 2023.
DOI: 10.1093/oso/9780197652398.003.0001

ambivalence about what to do, you might say, is an unwelcome (but not unexpected) companion in her deliberations.

Because the distress that we feel when we are in cases of this sort is often alarmingly pressing and anxiety inducing, it's tempting and, indeed, perhaps impossible not to regard the state of being ambivalent as bad. After all, when we are genuinely "of two minds" and experience our self as being torn, it seems that, necessarily, we are neither unified as agents nor wholehearted in our decisions. As such, we do not and, in fact, cannot fully stand behind our choices and subsequent behavior. But surely this is how we *should be* as agents, since when we are unified as an agent or wholehearted in our choices, we are freed from the terrible burdens that agents like Erica experience. That is, unity and wholeheartedness provide us with a particular kind of *freedom*—freedom from internal strife—which seems good in just the way ambivalence seems bad. When we are free in the way that is characteristic of wholeheartedness, we are not likely to be weighed down by anxiety or despair in response to our circumstances. Nor will we be prone to second-guessing our choices or feeling regret after we have made them. But freedom of this sort doesn't just consist in the *absence* of these sorts of bad pathologies; it has a positive component as well. When we are not divided but unified, and when we are not ambivalent but wholehearted, we can be content with ourselves and satisfied with our choices in an especially meaningful way. We can rest easy in the knowledge that what we do fully expresses who we are. We are, in a word, authentic.

But unity and wholeheartedness provide more than freedom. They also serve as the basis for another important agential good: *integrity*. The lack of unity and wholeheartedness that ambivalent agents experience is inherently destabilizing. We have it on good authority, after all, that "every kingdom divided against itself is laid waste, and no city or house divided against itself will stand."[1] But if this is correct—and it certainly seems to be in the

---

[1] Matthew 12:25 (ESV). This passage is also prominently featured in Abraham Lincoln's "A House Divided" speech (1858).

case of a political state that is embroiled in a civil war—then ambivalence is not merely something that we experience as a psychically distressing phenomenon. It is a genuine defect of one's agency. What this means is that ambivalence doesn't just prevent us from really feeling content with ourselves or taking satisfaction in our decisions. It also, and perhaps even more importantly, prevents us from being well-functioning agents.

## 1.2.  A Brief History of Ambivalence

At least, this is what we've been told throughout the Western philosophical tradition. In *Republic*, Plato critically discusses agents whose souls are divided in a way that is characteristic of ambivalence. Moreover, he famously links *unity* within the agent—i.e., harmony between the independent sources of motivation that comprise one's soul—with *justice* and, further, with his conception of the good life more generally (cf. *Republic* 352b5–d5, 434b5–c, etc.). Accordingly, the ambivalent agent, whose soul is unstable, at war with itself, and lacking in internal harmony, cannot be just. Being in such a state, however, is not simply bad in the way that one might ordinarily regard impediments to one's freedom as bad. That is, it's not just an unfortunate way of being that one can more or less work around. For Plato, such an agent is actually "*incapable of action* because of inner faction and not being of one mind with himself." His ambivalence, in other words, "make[s] him his own enemy" (*Republic* 352a5; emphasis added). To be a good agent, and indeed, by Plato's lights, to be a functioning agent at all requires us to have our souls structured in a way that eliminates ambivalence and instead secures unification.

Several centuries later, Augustine makes strikingly similar claims. According to Augustine, when our wills are fragmented (which they invariably are for all those who are not wholeheartedly resting in God's grace), we find ourselves in a "monstrous situation" in which "we are dealing with a morbid condition of the mind . . . [containing] two wills. Neither of them is complete, and what is present in the one is lacking in the other." This state, Augustine claims, renders us "dissociated" from ourselves and more importantly (given Augustine's conception of the Good), from God (*Confessions* VIII.Ix.21–22). Naturally, Augustine thinks, it isn't healthy for us to be alienated from ourselves (or potentially from God) in this way. An ambivalent mind, Augustine therefore concludes, threatens the proper functioning of our rational agency in the same way a potentially terminal disease threatens the proper functioning of our bodies.

However, Plato and Augustine are not the only philosophers who take ambivalence to be a direct threat to well-functioning agency: Descartes, Spinoza, and Kierkegaard all agree.[2] So too, Nietzsche suggests that maladies like ambivalence preclude one from being a "higher man."[3] More recently, contemporary action theorists like Harry Frankfurt (1988, 1992, 2004) and Christine M. Korsgaard (1999, 2009) have also agreed with Plato et al. that well-functioning agency requires wholeheartedness or a fully integrated practical identity.

Frankfurt articulates this point by claiming that "the mind is healthy—at least with respect to its volitional faculty—insofar as it is wholehearted" (Frankfurt 2004, 95). Frankfurt then contrasts an agent who is "healthy" with an agent who is ambivalent. (Notice here that Frankfurt's attempt to connect wholeheartedness with psychic health echoes not only Augustine but also Plato's account of justice in *Republic*.) Concerning the unhealthy, ambivalent agent, Frankfurt writes, "His will is unstable and incoherent, moving

---

[2] In *Meditations* IV Descartes suggests that a will that vacillates with respect to the good is less free. Spinoza laments the vacillation of our affects in *Ethics* III. And Kierkegaard supplies us with a series of arguments against the state of being "double-minded" in *Purity of the Heart Is to Will One Thing*.

[3] See Nietzsche's *The Gay Science* and *Thus Spoke Zarathustra*. I return to these arguments in Chapter 4.

him from contrary directions simultaneously or in a disorderly sequence" (Frankfurt 2004, 92).[4] And clearly, Frankfurt concludes, an agent's failure to wholeheartedly integrate his unstable and incoherent will is something to be avoided, since instability and incoherence are not—and *cannot* be—ideal ways to be constituted as an agent.

Unlike Augustine and Frankfurt, Korsgaard doesn't address the phenomenon of ambivalence explicitly. But this doesn't mean her theory of well-functioning agency has no implications for the status of ambivalent individuals—far from it, in fact. According to Korsgaard, activity as such is to be understood as a form of self-constitution (Korsgaard 1999, 2009). That is, for Korsgaard, what we are doing most fundamentally when we engage in *any* rational activity is engaging in the act of *making ourselves* as rational agents.[5] Accordingly, the goodness of any action is determined by how well the agent constitutes herself in virtue of choosing that action. What, then, is required to be a well-constituted agent? Like Plato, Korsgaard claims that a well-constituted agent is one who is fully integrated. By contrast, a poorly constituted agent is barely an agent at all. As a result, we fail to constitute ourselves well when we are ambivalent, since in such cases, our wills are divided in a way that precludes full integration. It therefore seems that on Korsgaard's

---

[4] Frankfurt (1971) identifies the agent's will with the first-order desire that is effective in moving her to act. On this understanding of the will, it seems that it cannot be "divided" in any meaningful sense. Accordingly, we're left with a somewhat puzzling claim here given Frankfurt's earlier account of the will. One possible explanation for Frankfurt's claim that the will can be unstable and incoherent is that *the agent herself* can be unstable and incoherent in virtue of being unsettled about which particular first-order desire (of a competing set) is her will. A second possibility is that Frankfurt comes to think of the will in a less narrow way. On this alternative picture, which is suggested throughout Frankfurt 2004, an agent's will is not her effective first-order desire in particular, but the volitional superstructure that organizes her cares and loves, and moves her to act. The interpretative difficulties that emerge in Frankfurt's discussions of the will notwithstanding, I am optimistic that we can make sense of the phenomenon he is identifying here.

[5] This is similar to Frankfurt's claim that "it is these acts of [resolving one's will]—that create a self out of the raw materials of inner life" (Frankfurt 1988, 170).

view, no choice made by an ambivalent agent can be unequivocally good.

Yet despite widespread, even *overwhelming* agreement about the badness of ambivalence among this otherwise motley yet extremely impressive assortment of unificationists, it is my view that ambivalence as such is no threat to well-functioning agency. The fact that an agent fails to be fully integrated, lacks purity of heart, or is less than wholehearted in her choices tells us nothing about whether she is well-functioning as an agent. Moreover, I contend that in many cases wholeheartedness is itself a defect in an agent's will. For example, if an agent wholeheartedly endorses one of her conflicting motives or concerns over the other without sufficient justification, it is plausible that in that case, she is not being appropriately responsive to rational considerations. She is not, in other words, exercising her *normative competence*. Accordingly, in that moment, she is not well-functioning agent.

This, of course, does not mean that *all* instances of wholeheartedness issue from a defective will. Nor does it mean that no cases of ambivalence can be bad for our agency. It also does not mean we should always relish the experience of being ambivalent or its consequences for us as rational agents. It does entail, though, that we have nothing to fear from ambivalence as such, and that it gives us no reason to doubt ourselves as well-functioning agents even in times of severe disunity.[6]

---

[6] In developing the anti-unificationist themes of this book, I stand with a number of other philosophers who have suggested, if not explicitly claimed, that they also reject elements of the unificationist tradition's emphasis on unity or wholeheartedness. These philosophers attack unificationist commitments from a variety of perspectives: from both feminist and mestiza concerns about traditional conceptions of identity and autonomy; from medical ethicist worries about resolving difficult choices; and from pluralist theories of value. See Gloria Anzaldúa (1987); Cheshire Calhoun (1995); Susan Wolf (2002); Edwina Barvosa (2007, 2008); Jacqui Poltera (2011); Logi Gunnarsson (2014), Hili Razinsky (2017), and Simon Feldman and Allan Hazlitt (2021) for a representative sample.

Now, I want to be clear here. In suggesting that ambivalence can be valuable, or that even ideal, well-functioning agents might very well be ambivalent, I am not merely suggesting that there is some *instrumental* value in being ambivalent. This point is not controversial. Indeed, Frankfurt himself concedes it, telling us that "accepting ambivalence may sometimes be healthy or wise" (Frankfurt 1992, 11). In other words, even unificationists can admit that if being ambivalent would help you cope with a difficult decision or transition in your life better than being wholehearted would, then you have grounds for embracing ambivalence. Of course, these theorists are also quick to claim that we shouldn't let the *efficacy* or *utility* of ambivalence as a coping mechanism be the basis of a genuine claim about its intrinsic value or about its place in the truly well-functioning agent. In other words, for unificationists like Frankfurt, your therapist might rightly counsel ambivalence, but your moral psychologist never should.

By contrast, I am offering a much stronger claim about the nature of well-functioning agency. On my view, ambivalence is often the *fitting* or *proper* response to the practical conflict that an agent faces. And the reason for this is simple: given the real and oftentimes insuperable conflicts that can occur between agents' values, commitments, or concerns, it is ambivalence rather than wholeheartedness that manifests normative competence on the part of the agent. This follows from a more general conception of what makes us well-functioning agents. According to this view, we do well qua agents when we are responsive to good things, and to the reasons there are to pursue, realize, promote, honor, protect, respect, and maintain those things. Volitional health is thus not to be understood in terms of agential unity or wholeheartedness. Instead, we should regard as healthy someone whose will is structured in a way that is suitably sensitive to the good things that matter to her. But given the diverse patterns of values and concerns that we all have, this conception of well-functioning agency allows for and indeed often calls for openness to ambivalence on our parts.

To that end, this book is an invitation to action theorists and moral psychologists to reorient their theories. We should no longer treat ambivalence, division, lack of unity, or impurity of heart as bogeymen. As it happens, fragmentation in one's volitional commitments is often intrinsically important. For though whole-heartedness can sometimes be advisable as a coping mechanism—it is, after all, sometimes just psychologically easier to deal with a con-flict between two things that matter to you by dissociating yourself from one of those things—the wholehearted agent less frequently manifests a suitable degree of normative competence in the face of practical conflict.[7] But this is not true of the properly ambivalent agent. Her will is the one that has a healthy and appropriate grasp on the axiological complexity that faces us in our lives.

## 1.3.  Outline of the Book

In what follows, I will argue for these claims. In Part I, I seek to clarify the nature of ambivalence (Chapter 2) and then consider and respond to a series of unificationist arguments (Chapters 3–6). This portion of the book is focused exclusively on trying to recon-struct and respond to arguments of the sort that unificationists like Plato, Augustine, Frankfurt, and Korsgaard (among others) com-monly use in defense of their accounts of well-functioning agency. The positive portion of the book can be found in Part II, where I set out new arguments in defense of being ambivalent. There I'll specif-ically argue that well-functioning agency regularly requires that we be susceptible to ambivalence (Chapters 7–9). With this very "big

---

[7] Cases of ambivalence that J. S. Blumenthal-Barby (2021) calls "paralyzing ambiv-alence" might be instances of the sort of practical conflict in which one has powerful instrumental grounds for becoming wholehearted.

picture" overview in mind, I now want to consider at some level of granularity the core topics of the book. I cannot, of course, discuss all of the details here, but I nevertheless hope that this will give you what you need to get started and, if possible, whet your appetite for what's to come.

### 1.3.1. Part I: A House Divided

To begin Part I, I develop an account of ambivalence that both specifies how it arises and distinguishes it from other related phenomena. Ambivalence arises when an agent finds herself conflicted about what to do in a particular way. Specifically, the ambivalent agent finds that the motives or values that are most central to who she is as an agent are in opposition with one another. What this means is that ambivalence, unlike indecision, uncertainty, or the vague feeling of being unsettled that we all sometimes have, implicates the innermost elements of our practical selves. Additionally, I argue that there is a distinctive *qualitative* element to ambivalence. When we are ambivalent, we feel as if we are unable to proceed without giving up something of significant value. In other words, the ambivalent agent experiences her practical conflict as one in which there will be some significant *value remainder* no matter how she chooses. Finally, I consider two specific varieties of ambivalence that can occur, and how each of these puts constraints on what the agent must do if she wants to free herself from her ambivalence, as unificationists insist she should.

After clarifying the nature of ambivalence, I turn to a trio of unificationist arguments. The first of these, which will be the subject of Chapter 3, is the *Resolution Argument*. According to this argument, we are able to fully resolve our wills in cases of practical conflict only if we come to wholeheartedly identify with one of the conflicting motives (as well as the course of action that that motive rationalizes). The reason for this is that in the absence of whole-hearted resolution with respect to one of our conflicting motives, the motive that in fact moves us to act lacks normative or action-guiding authority. Because it lacks wholehearted endorsement, such a motive would be effective only because it is stronger than its counterpart. But "might doesn't make right" in politics or in practical agency. What's needed for authority or legitimacy in each case is consent or endorsement.

If, on the other hand, I wholeheartedly resolve myself to be moved by this motive rather than its counterpart, I endorse the former's authority to guide my behavior while thereby stripping the latter motive of its normative authority. This allows the former motive to guide my will and rationalize my behavior. But it is crucial for our *autonomy* or *self-governance* that we are able to resolve our wills in this way—that we are moved by the motives we endorse and not simply by those that exert the most psychological force. As a result, the Resolution Argument concludes that we cannot maintain ambivalence in the face of practical conflict.

The unificationist argument that I consider in Chapter 4 is the *Affirmation Argument*. This argument begins with a Nietzschean premise according to which our choices are meaningful for us only if we can wholeheartedly affirm them. This premise emerges from the invitation for reflection that Nietzsche offers us in *Gay Science* 341. There he asks us to consider how we would respond to a demon who informs us that everything we do will be replayed again and again for all eternity. Would the prospect of that be the greatest weight you can imagine? Or would it instead fill you with joy and a sense of satisfaction? If the former, it seems that you are *dissatisfied* with your life in a fundamental way. If the latter, then it seems that you regard your life as *meaningful* in a distinctive way. Yet when we are ambivalent we are not able to fully affirm our motives or choices considered individually or our lives considered as a whole. Therefore, the ambivalent life cannot be uniquely meaningful in the way it is possible for a wholehearted life to be.

The final unificationist argument, discussed in Chapters 5 and 6, has historically been the argument that most powerfully motivates the view that ambivalence is an agential failing. This argument, the *Argument from Self-Defeat*, is in fact a family of related arguments, each of which identifies a way in which divisions in one's will (or *soul* to put the point in more Platonic terms) threaten the meaningful possibility of *integrity*. For Plato, a soul that finds itself directed by competing, mutually incompatible motivational impulses is at war with itself, in just the same way a city with two (or more) apparently authoritative rulers who wanted to enact incompatible laws is at war with itself. But just as this sort of political conflict would render a city insufficiently stable to really count as a single political body, so too, volitional conflicts of the sort that are characteristic of ambivalence would deeply undercut the ordinary ways in which we regard ourselves as agents. Korsgaard (1999, 2009) argues for a similar conclusion, when she claims that the agent who fails to unify herself thereby fails, at least to some degree, in the activity of constituting herself as an agent. On this version of the argument, ambivalence is *literally* self-defeating, in that it precludes the form of *self-constitution* that Korsgaard regards as the sine qua non of integrity.

Frankfurt (1999, 2004) argues for this point slightly differently. For Frankfurt, ambivalence is self-defeating in the same way that holding incompatible beliefs is self-defeating. If I believe that p and that ~p, then I guarantee that I believe something false, and I fail to give myself a rational basis on which to make decisions about what to do. Similarly, Erica's ambivalence pulls her in competing and incompatible directions. She therefore guarantees that she will be incoherent as an agent. In other words, her failure to whole-heartedly endorse one of the competing motivational impulses "precludes behavioral effectiveness" (Frankfurt 2004, 96), and so, the unificationists conclude, it defeats the whole "point" of being an agent, which is to translate one's motivations and values into action without violating the integrity of our practical selves.

## 1.3.2. Part II: A Wise Inconsistency

In Chapters 3–6, I will be primarily concerned with showing that these unificationist arguments fail to secure their conclusions. Yet for all that I say in those chapters, ambivalence might still be the agential malady that unificationists allege, if not for the reasons they suspect. Accordingly, the task of the second part of the book is to offer positive arguments on behalf of ambivalence as being a key agential good.

To that end, in Chapter 7 I turn directly to the question of what is required for well-functioning agency. Unlike the more elaborate theories of agency favored by unificationists—e.g., that the aim of agency is to unify the agent, or to be wholehearted, or to consti-tute the agent—I propose a simple constraint on well-functioning agency, which is simply that a well-functioning agent will be sensi-tive, attuned, and responsive to the reasons for action that she has. In other words, a person is a well-functioning agent only insofar as her decisions and subsequent behavior issue from exercises of her normative competence. This constraint on well-functioning agency is weak enough that any plausible conception of well-functioning agency can accommodate it. And yet, I will argue, it is sufficient to explain why ambivalence can be good for its own sake.

To develop this point, I introduce and discuss a specific class of reasons for actions that agents often have, which I call *countervolitional reasons*. Countervolitional reasons are, in es-sence, reasons to have done otherwise. So, for example, in Erica's case, if we suppose for the sake of argument that she chooses to take the job opportunity rather than continuing as caregiver for her parents, the reasons she had for opting for the latter option are countervolitional, since they ran counter to how she actually chose. In supposing that Erica takes the new job, we are supposing that Erica thought that the reasons for opting for that option ultimately outweighed those for staying close to loved ones (at least insofar as we're not imaging her to be acting irrationally). Yet the fact that she should all-things-considered take the job doesn't mean that she has *no reason at all* to stay behind. In fact, she has powerful reasons to stay behind—it's just that, as we're imagining it, these reasons are ultimately outweighed. But surely the fact that Erica has especially weighty countervolitional reasons in this case means that she has reason to pursue her chosen end in a different fashion than she would if she lacked those reasons altogether (say, a case in which her parents were hardy and hale).

In particular, we'll see, these considerations rationalize a high measure of unwillingness on Erica's part to leave in a way that finally and unequivocally cuts off her family. So too, her weighty countervolitional reasons rationalize a willingness to be as flexible in how she proceeds further in her career. This suggests that for Erica, these reasons, which are so weighty because of her deep love for her parents, still have an important role to play in shaping and structuring Erica's overall set of priorities and deliberative orientation. That is, though they are outweighed in the circumstances, they seem to retain no small amount of normative authority for Erica. But this is just to say that in virtue of her continued sensitivity, attunement, and responsiveness to these reasons, Erica steadfastly maintains her ambivalence.

Notice that in this case, Erica's unwillingness to wholeheartedly embrace her decision looks less like an impediment to freedom or integrity and more like a manifestation of her normative competence. It therefore looks like well-functioning agency, which must surely involve the exercise of normative competence, sometimes requires agents not be unified or wholehearted but be ambivalent.

Now you might be worried that ultimately, this is a very weak conclusion. Perhaps cases in which well-functioning agency requires ambivalence are exceedingly rare, or perhaps the reasons to be ambivalent are exceptionally weak, such that ordinarily we are free to simply ignore them. If so, then wholeheartedness might still be preferable as a regulative ideal of well-functioning agency, even if it is suboptimal in a small set of cases. In Chapter 8, I take the teeth out of this unificationist response by arguing that cases in which we should be ambivalent are, if not ubiquitous, utterly ordinary for any agent who is concerned with either morality or with living a good or meaningful life. This is the *Regularity Argument*.

In support of this argument, I consider a variety of ways in which morality often forces us to wrestle with extremely difficult trade-offs. Should you remove this person from the ventilator because their quality of life and life expectancy is low in order to try to save someone who is more likely to have better health outcomes? Should you opt for palliative care rather than treatment? Should you find out whether your fetus tests positive for a slate of genetic conditions? And if so, should you abort the fetus or carry it to term? Should you continue to support someone who has helped you greatly but who has also treated others in despicable ways? Should you keep a promise if you find out that it will end up causing a not insignificant amount of harm?

These are, it seems to me, extremely difficult questions. So difficult, in fact, that W. D. Ross (1930), who did as much as anyone to articulate the variety of ways in which different deontic goods can come into conflict, wasn't sure that we could ever know which of our so-called "prima facie duties" ultimately wins the day. Yet even supposing that there is a correct answer as to what an agent is morally (and perhaps rationally) required to do in each of these trade-off situations *and she knows* that answer, there is still significant room for merited ambivalence in most, if not all, of these cases. This point also holds in the case of many of the virtues. Insofar as we have moral grounds for cultivating virtuous dispositions, we'll have reason to develop dispositions that will, in quite a wide variety of circumstances, put us at war with ourselves. We see this clearly in the case of specific interpersonal virtues—virtues like generosity, love, mercifulness, and courage, to name a few.

The regularity of ambivalence-meriting conflicts perhaps becomes even clearer when we turn to the standards for living a good or meaningful life. A good life paradigmatically requires inter alia a minimal diversity in an individual's pattern of concerns. It's not usually enough for a meaningful life that someone really identifies exclusively and wholeheartedly with, for example, their philosophical activity. Even if this person is truly among the greats—a living Mengzi or Avicenna or Wollstonecraft—and so living an important or significant philosophical life, if they failed to maintain at least a minimal ability to relate well with others or in navigating their environments, then it's doubtful that they could be said to be living a good life—i.e., a life that is *good for them*. And of course, very few of us are among the greats in any endeavor, so for us, this point's bite is even harder. If I, a second- or third-rate philosopher (at best), identify exclusively with my philosophical activity to the exclusion of caring about anything else, then though I will be able to pursue "the life of the mind" unequivocally, it just seems clear that I wouldn't be living a good or particularly meaningful life. Maybe there is some value to being thoroughly swept away in the life of a middling mind. But I suspect that it's really only in tandem with a variety of other concerns and values and pursuits that the import of philosophical activity contributes positively to how well my life goes or how meaningful it ultimately is.

What this means is that once I recognize that to live well, I must be deeply invested in a fairly wide variety of projects and activities, it becomes clear that, so too, I must be open to experiencing ambivalence. After all, it is precisely this sort of situation that leads to Erica's practical conflict. She is a loving daughter who cares deeply for her parents and for materially supporting them at this stage of their lives. But she is also a creative and ambitious person, who has quite reasonably invested a lot of herself into her work. The diversity of her activities seem precisely what it is in virtue of which she is living a full and rich life. But these activities are also precisely the source of her ambivalence in the face of a practical conflict that pits one of her concerns against the other. Rather than facilitating a life well lived, the desire to be wholehearted would push us to abandon one of these pursuits in an effort to make ourselves into a coherent whole. At the abstract level of philosophical theorizing, this has the illusory air of being a worthy ideal for which to strive. But, as I hope becomes clear by the conclusion of Chapter 8, the actual condition of being human tells a different story.

# PART I

# A HOUSE DIVIDED

Every kingdom divided against itself is laid wasted,
and no city or house divided against itself will stand.
—Matthew 12:25

# 2

# Ambivalence

## 2.1. Varieties of Personal Conflict

Before getting to the question of what exactly ambivalence is, we must distinguish it from a class of closely related phenomena, each of which emerges in the face of a difficult decision about what to do. Erica's dilemma, for example, leaves her ambivalent as to how she should proceed, but it surely engenders other feelings as well. She probably feels like she cannot make up her mind, as though she is continuously going back and forth over the options. Accordingly, she might describe herself as being *indecisive*. She might also feel in the moment as if she's inclined one way rather than another, but not be completely confident that she's right. In such a case, she might be either unsure of what her preferences really are or how to best weigh them against one another. If this is how she's feeling, then she might describe herself as *uncertain* or *unsettled* about what to do. It's also possible that Erica has fully settled on what she's going to do, but then, when the moment comes to execute her choice, she lacks the courage of her convictions. Here, she might be thought of as *wavering* (if it's still possible that she'll follow her convictions), or, if she acts contrary to her best judgment, she might instead be better characterized as *weak-willed*. But maybe Erica has decided what to do, and although she is not wavering, she still feels the pull of the alternative option. Here, she seems to have *mixed feelings*.

Each of these states—indecision, uncertainty, feeling unsettled, wavering in one's convictions, weakness of will, and mixed feelings—is, at least in my own experience, familiar, and dispiriting in just the ways that we typically associate with ambivalence. And

*In Praise of Ambivalence*. D. Justin Coates, Oxford University Press. © Oxford University Press 2023.
DOI: 10.1093/oso/9780197652398.003.0002

as described here, many of these states are so deeply entwined with ambivalence that it's not easy to perspicuously distinguish them. If, for example, you asked Erica about the state she finds herself in, she might describe herself as being "indecisive," "uncertain," "unsettled," "wavering," "weak-willed," or as "having mixed feelings" just as readily as she would describe herself as simply being ambivalent, given that in ordinary usage, ambivalence often connotes that these other states are present as well.

No doubt Erica's feelings in this case reflect a real truth, that in many paradigm cases of ambivalence we are also indecisive, uncertain, conflicted, wavering, and experiencing mixed feelings. And in many cases as well, we are even weak-willed. But conceptually, I contend, these phenomena are distinct. To sort this out, I want to think about some specific cases of personal conflict. These cases will highlight ways in which ambivalence and these related phenomena are distinct forms of personal conflict. Yet they do so in a way that, I hope, fully acknowledges that for human agents, these ambivalence and these phenomena regularly co-vary and are frequently mutually reinforcing.

\* \* \*

To begin, I want to consider Arthur Dimmesdale, a protagonist in Nathaniel Hawthorne's *The Scarlet Letter*. The case of Dimmesdale is an especially interesting one because he is doubly ambivalent. He is in the first place torn between his love for God and continuing in his station as God's vicar in colonial New England. The former motive—his love for God—propels him to publicly confess his affair with Hester Prynne. By contrast, the latter motive—founded not exclusively in a desire for self-preservation but also in his true concern for his parishioners' welfare—drives him to continue in his role as their spiritual counselor (he is, we see, quite good at it). However, his ambivalence does not stop here. He is also torn between a longing for a self-destructive form of atonement for his sin and the love that he "consecrated" with Hester. His longing for atonement drives him toward self-abnegation, which inter alia involves a denial of what he genuinely shared with Hester. But of course, his love for her, and also for Pearl, their daughter, seeks acknowledgment as well.

Dimmesdale is undoubtedly conflicted. He vacillates between boldly announcing himself to his parishioners on the one hand and conveying with certainty to Pearl that he will only do so on Judgment Day, when every other tongue confesses as well. He desperately wants to receive proper punishment for his sin—not the self-inflicted simulacrum of punishment he suffers at his own hand but genuine retribution from an appropriate judge. Despite this, he cannot bring himself to reveal the truth and be condemned. He also loves Hester but makes himself refuse her invitation to flee the colony. If anyone is ambivalent, it is Dimmesdale. And yet his ambivalence seems ineluctably caught up with the fact that he is also indecisive, uncertain, lacking in the courage of his convictions, and weak-willed.

It is precisely because of cases like Dimmesdale's that it is so easy to run together ambivalence and other varieties of being personally conflicted. Yet for all that, none of these states is *necessary* for ambivalence. This is easiest to see in the case of indecisiveness or of being unsure what to do. It seems quite possible, after all, to be *certain* about what one should do and yet still be ambivalent. Dimmesdale himself eventually comes to sincerely believe he must reveal himself not on Judgment Day but many, many days before, and yet this does little—at least initially—to undercut his ambivalence about doing so.

Similarly, you don't need to be wavering or weak-willed in your commitment to a selected course of action in order to be ambivalent. In Arthur Dimmesdale's particular case, of course, his decision to publicly confess puts to rest not only years of wavering and weakness but also his ambivalence. This suggests these phenomena are inextricably linked. But it is not a necessary consequence of his decision to confess before the town's elders and accept his ignominious death that he resolves his ambivalence. Undoubtedly, Dimmesdale could have maintained the courage of his convictions by revealing his status as an adulterer while simultaneously maintaining his ambivalence. In other words, he could have settled his will, and as a result, ended his wavering and weakness without *thereby* ending his ambivalence.

This possibility explains what is so disappointing about Dimmesdale's final words to Hester: the *lack* of ambivalence they express.

> "Hush, Hester, hush!" said he, with tremulous solemnity. "The law we broke!—the sin here so awfully revealed!—let these alone be in thy thoughts! I fear! I fear! It may be, that, when we forgot our God,—when we violated our reverence for the other's soul,— it was thenceforth vain to hope that we could meet hereafter, in an everlasting and pure reunion." (199)

As I see it, the problem with this farewell is that Dimmesdale could, and perhaps *should*, have insisted on revealing the truth—as he honestly believed he must—without having fully freed himself of the tension that had its source in his love for Hester and his desire to be with her. That is, it's hard not to want Dimmesdale to find peace, but it's also hard not to want for him to give Hester her due. But when he eliminates his ambivalence, Dimmesdale is no longer willing to even hope that he and Hester could be united in a meaningful way. And this full-scale rejection of that aspect of who he is disheartening.[1] Of course, this disappointment only makes sense if Dimmesdale *could* have acted unwaveringly from the courage of his convictions and yet maintained his psychic fragmentation. So while the experiences of being wavering or weak-willed seem to be

---

[1] It's hard not to see this as an implicit rejection on Hawthorne's part of the overly narrow conception of goodness accepted by New England Puritans.

regular companions with ambivalence, as they are in Dimmesdale's case, they cannot be necessary for ambivalence.

The states of indecision, uncertainty, lacking the courage of one's convictions, or suffering from weakness of will are not *sufficient* for ambivalence either. After all, it's obviously the case that one *should* be undecided or uncertain about what to do in many cases, particularly cases in which one lacks good evidence as to what to do next. But the fact that I'm unsure of what to do next when I can't, for example, make sense of IKEA's assembly instructions doesn't mean that I'm ambivalent about what to do. Nor does it mean that my agency is somehow defective. Perhaps it means is that I'm bad at reading directions. Or it might mean that IKEA is bad at producing them. In either case, the deficiency, if there is indeed one, is ultimately an *epistemic* one rather than an *agential* one. After all, it isn't my will that fails in this case; rather, it is either a failure in my capacity for understanding, or in IKEA's ability to helpfully transmit information.

Similarly, the fact that an agent's desires are unsettled does not suffice for ambivalence. I might be uncertain about (or vacillating between) whether to finish working on this paragraph or go get lunch right now, since I currently want to do both. But this conflict doesn't entail that my will is torn or that I am in danger of betraying myself. Nor does this kind of personal conflict seem to carry the existential weight that we ordinarily attach to ambivalence. Instead, the fact that I am uncertain about what to do and slightly wavering in this case simply means that I have not decided what I'm going to do. Clearly, however, being undecided as I am in this and in many related cases (e.g., when I'm looking at a menu, when I'm unsure of what to get my wife for her birthday, when I'm thinking about where to go for my next vacation, etc.) is not enough for ambivalence. The reason for this is that *I'll* be okay regardless of whether I choose to keep working or go get some lunch. My practical self is, in other words, resilient with respect to how I choose here. But ambivalence feels so distressing precisely because we worry that our practical selves aren't resilient to the sorts of conflicts that are characteristic of ambivalence. This suggests that simply being uncertain about every little thing isn't enough for ambivalence.

Last, we must again consider the close connection between weakness and ambivalence. Already we've seen that weakness is not necessary for ambivalence. But does it suffice? The answer is again, I think, clearly no. Consider, for example, that in some cases of ambivalence, the agent finds herself torn between two courses of action that are roughly on a par with one another.[2] This is true, for example, of Erica. Given her values and commitments—given who she is—neither option is clearly better. After significant deliberation, Erica might form a judgment that one course of action rather than the other one is ultimately better. But then again, she might not. Yet if she does not, then clearly ambivalence on her part does not flow from weakness of will, since in such cases, Erica may not make any all-things-considered judgment as to which option should be pursued (and indeed, there might be no fact of the matter about which to judge) to which she fails to conform her behavior.[3]

However, many other cases of ambivalence do involve an agent divided over two courses of action that the agent herself judges to be very different in their reasonableness (Dimmesdale plausibly falls in this category, since he thinks it would undoubtedly be better for him to publicly confess). In these sorts of cases, in which an

[2] This means that some cases of ambivalence are "hard choices" as Ruth Chang (2017) defines them. However, not all cases of ambivalence will be "hard" in Chang's sense, since not all cases of ambivalence involve a conflict between concerns that point us to outcomes that are "on a par."

[3] There is an even more straightforward argument that weakness is insufficient for ambivalence. It is possible, I submit, to imagine a weak-willed agent who is not motivated *at all* to pursue the course of action she regards as optimal. But clearly this agent, who is in no way pulled toward one alternative, will not be ambivalent about her choice between these alternatives, even though she recognizes that she should be doing something else. Of course, motivational internalists will deny precisely the premise that one can judge a course of action to be best or optimal and not be motivated at least to some degree. That's why the official argument on offer in this passage does not rest on controversial claims about the necessary connections (or lack thereof) between evaluative judgments and human motivation.

agent believes that one course of action is clearly better than another, she is frequently, though by no means exclusively, disposed (often to some significant degree) to pursue the one she judges to be best. Yet in cases of weakness of will, she acts contrary to that judgment. So the weak-willed agent must also have felt some strong pull toward the course of action that, by her lights, is worse than an available alternative. This motive moved her to act, after all! In these cases, then, we will typically find agents who are genuinely divided and subsequently ambivalent about their personal conflict, since a judgment they regard as sound pulls them one way and a deep attraction to an alternative pulls them in a contrary way.

This kind of weakness/ambivalence hybrid is discussed not only in Hawthorne's *The Scarlet Letter*[4] but also in Augustine's *Confessions*[5] and, before that, in St. Paul's reflections on the difficulty of conforming himself to (what he regards as) God's law. In one striking passage on the topic of the ongoing internal conflict between his mind and his flesh, Paul describes his propensity for weakness—"For I do not do the good I want to do, but the evil I do not want to do—this I keep on doing"—as itself being an expression of his ambivalence. In particular, he identifies the following pattern:

[4] Dimmesdale "long[s] to speak out, from his own pulpit, at the full height of his voice, and tell the people what he was" (113), and yet he cannot bring himself to do this. He is weak, and in his weakness, it seems, he is ambivalent, since his desire to conceal his wrongdoing is also one that is at the heart of who he is as an agent.

[5] Recall Augustine's prayer that "God make [him] chaste, but not yet." In feeling as if he needed to make this request of God, Augustine reveals that he thinks chastity is preferable to promiscuity and also that he is more strongly attracted to the latter than to the former. This means that insofar as he is unable to be chaste, he is weak-willed. But notice also that while his prayer shows him to care about his sex life to a great degree, how he feels about that is not unequivocal. He identifies with his judgment that chastity is deeply important to living well so thoroughly that he is pleading with God to help him change what matters to him. Augustine thus cares deeply about sexual pleasure but also wants very much to not care about such pursuits. This reveals Augustine to be not only weak-willed but also ambivalent. It's natural to conclude, then, that these phenomena are very much of a piece with one another.

> So I find this law at work: Although I want to do good, evil is right
> there with me. For in my inner being I delight in God's law; but
> I see another law at work in me, waging war against the law of my
> mind and making me a prisoner of the law of sin at work within
> me. What a wretched man I am! (Romans 7:19, 21–24; New
> International Version)

Paul wants to be moved exclusively by God's commands. Yet he
finds within himself another law. He does not fully affirm his allegiance to this law in what he says—he regards it as imprisoning
him—and yet he does give allegiance to it to some degree insofar as
he regards his sinful activity as being genuinely his own. Paul thus
seems to be divided between sinful motives that he recognizes as
his own, and "higher" motives that he explicitly affirms, even as he
falls short of them. He wants to do good and then fails to do so. He
is, in other words, both weak-willed and ambivalent.

But while many cases of weakness do involve ambivalence in just
the way Paul alludes to (and that is later present in both Augustine's
and Dimmesdale's cases), it's dubious that all or even most cases
of weakness are connected to ambivalence in any meaningful
way. When I stay on the couch to watch a football game featuring
teams I don't care about ("Coming up! The 2-6 Cincinnati Bengals
are going to take on the 4-4 Arizona Cardinals") instead of doing
the grading I know I should be doing, I'm weak-willed. And I'm
lazy. And I'm self-indulgent. But despite all this, I'm not ambivalent. There's no internal tension or agony on my part. I'm not, for
example, worried about damaging my practical self in any way if
I were to miss the game. Nor do I imagine there to be anything significant about my "dilemma" at all. I simply want to keep on lying
around, and I'm too weak (or too lazy or self-centered) to coun-
teract that desire's seductive inertia. Yet even this is enough to show
that it is simply a mistake to think weakness of will suffices for
ambivalence.

An admittedly more complicated case is that of "mixed feelings." When we describe ourselves as having mixed feelings, we are often *trying* to describe our ambivalence in a more or less precise way.[6] For this reason, I think the distinction between mixed feelings and ambivalence is murkier than is the distinction between ambivalence and indecision, uncertainty, wavering, and weakness. Despite this, I think there is an important distinction to be made. As a first pass at making it, I'll simply note that the category of mixed feelings seems much broader than the category of ambivalence. For example, one might have mixed feelings about watching the NFL, or about listening to the music of an abuser, or about paying taxes to a government that regularly engages in horrific malfeasance. It's possible that these conflicts of feeling and emotion are extremely difficult for you to manage, given your values. But the conflict that you experience in cases of mixed feelings might also be slight or superficial, as is the case when you have mixed feelings about your friend's new haircut: you like it somewhat but you also don't. However, ambivalence isn't superficial in this way; as I'll argue below, ambivalence has its source in the deepest elements of our practical selves.

A more significant difference between mixed feelings and ambivalence concerns the role of agency in both generating and resolving personal conflicts. We are largely passive with respect to the "feelings" that can sometimes be mixed. Indeed, they need not be reflective of our agency in any deep way. This is particularly true in the case of feelings that internalize others' take on us, like shame, for instance. So, for example, someone might feel shame about her body because it doesn't reflect cultural beauty standards. The same person might also love her body. In such a case, the person has conflicting emotions and, so, experiences "mixed feelings."

[6] See, e.g., Patricia Greenspan (1980), who defines ambivalence in terms of conflicting emotions. It might be that my disagreement with Greenspan on this point is merely terminological. We're both trying to identify related phenomena that we take to have philosophical import, but Greenspan is particularly interested in emotional conflicts, whereas I am concerned with volitional ones.

But this does not guarantee ambivalence. The person might regard the feelings of shame as not really reflecting her real assessment or "take." She might think, in other words, that the shameful feelings in question happen merely as a result of unendorsed cultural baggage. This person might therefore experience no ambivalence in deciding what to wear or in what or how much to eat because the emotional conflict she experiences is not one that directly implicates her *will*.

By contrast, in cases of ambivalence, the conflict that emerges has it source in our will, and so we cannot be passive with respect to the sources of the conflict. If I find myself with mixed feelings about something, I can simply shrug off one feeling—perhaps acknowledging its existence but not treating it as action-guiding to any real degree. In cases of ambivalence, however, this doesn't seem possible. With Erica, to return to that earlier example, we see an agent whose problem seems to be deeply intertwined with the fact that she does not and indeed cannot simply regard either her love for her parents or concern for self-realization as being something she can shrug off, ignoring its significance for her life.

Of course, it's undoubtedly true that Erica has mixed feelings, and that they are distressing and difficult to deal with in more or less the same way that we often regard ambivalence to be distressing and difficult to deal with. But very plausibly, Erica's conflicting emotions are themselves generated by prior *volitional* commitments on her part. That is, it's precisely because she endorses both her love of her parents and her desire to realize her goals that she feels the emotions she does. The new career opportunity threatens her relationship with her parents, and so she feels anxiety and worry. But it's also life-altering, and so she feels excited at the prospect of following her dreams. However, because these mixed feelings surely emerge from her prior ambivalence, they cannot be identified with it.

* * *

Of course, the fact that indecision, uncertainty, wavering, having mixed feelings, and weakness are distinct from ambivalence shouldn't lead us to conclude that these phenomena aren't central to the experience of ambivalence. It might be a mistake to identify any of these phenomena with ambivalence, but it's not a *silly* mistake. Yet these states are not ambivalence, and for reasons that I plan to make clear below, we'd do well to remember that.

As I'll understand it, then, what's distinctive about ambivalence is that it is necessary *inner* division that the agent experiences as not being resolvable without *value remainder* (or *value residue*).[7] But this pithy-yet-jargon-laden statement of the view hardly suffices. Accordingly, in the remainder of this chapter, I will be developing this account of ambivalence in greater detail. While I'm doing so, I'll connect it with previous attempts to make sense of both what inner division is and why it has practical significance. I conceive of this account as not being wholly unique but as building on and improving upon other standard understandings of ambivalence. With this road map in mind, let's return to a crucial source for understanding human agency: Plato's moral psychology.

## 2.2. The Problem of Inner Faction

In *Republic* 352a5, Plato tells us that *inner* faction renders us at war with ourselves, and that this particular kind of conflict necessarily frustrates our agency.[8] Given the frustration that so often comes

---

[7] In requiring the conflict to be located in the innermost elements of the self, I am relying on a distinction that goes back at least to Plato but which has been revived among analytic philosophers by Harry Frankfurt (1988): a distinction between *internal* states, which are the agent's own, and *external* states, which are mere causal forces that operate on the agent. In Frankfurt's wake, many others have usefully employed this distinction (see J. David Velleman [1992], David Shoemaker [2003], Agnieszka Jaworska [2007], among others).

I am also relying here on the idea of "value remainder," which goes back at least as far as the Greek tragedians, though again, it too has been revived in contemporary philosophy by Bernard Williams (1981), Martha Nussbaum (2001), and Patricia Greenspan (1995), among others.

[8] What I say here about Plato's moral psychology in *Republic* is not meant to be a novel interpretation. Indeed, my understanding of that text is heavily indebted to Julia Annas (1981), Martha Nussbaum (2001), Terrence Irwin (1995), , and C. D. C. Reeve (2004).

with ambivalence, it already seems very plausible that whatever else ambivalence might be, it is a kind of inner faction. Naturally, cases of ambivalence will not exhaust all varieties of inner faction that Plato concerns himself with. But even so, inner faction is surely *necessary* for ambivalence. As a result, Plato's treatment of inner faction seems to be a good place to start forming a clearer account of the phenomena in question. With that in mind the following questions seem especially pressing: What is inner faction? How does it arise? Do just any practical conflicts count as inner faction? And finally, what is the connection between inner faction and ambivalence?

Plato's own answer to the first of these questions flows from his tripartite anthropology. Our souls, he famously tells us, have three parts: reason, spirit, and appetite. And they are just—i.e., harmonious, healthy, well functioning, etc.—only if each of these parts is fulfilling its proper role within the individual. This suggests that every instance of disharmony that occurs within the soul must be damaging to the health and integrity of the individual. Yet this does not mean that all cases of disharmony are equally destructive. Indeed, Plato himself implies strongly that some conflicts occurring within the soul do very little to threaten the overall health of the individual. We can glean this implication by carefully attending to Plato's treatment of justice in the city.

Speaking of the city earlier in *Republic* Book IV, Socrates invites his interlocutor Glaucon to consider two types of conflicts that might occur. First:

> If a carpenter attempts to do the work of a shoemaker, or a shoemaker that of a carpenter, or they exchange their tools or honors with one another, or if the same person tries to do both jobs, and all other such exchanges are made, do you think that does any great harm to the city? (434a)

And second:

But I imagine that when someone who is, by nature, a craftsman or some other sort of moneymaker is puffed up by wealth, or by having a majority of votes, or by his own strength, or by some other such thing, and attempts to enter the class of soldiers; or when one of the soldiers who is unworthy to do so tries to enter that of judge and guardian and these exchange their tools and honors; or when the same person tries to do all these things at once, then I imagine you will agree that these exchanges and this meddling destroy the city. (434a5–b5)

In response the first of these scenarios, Glaucon flatly denies that meddling of this type has any real significance for the overall health of the city, and Socrates agrees. But as Socrates suspects, Glaucon also accepts that the sort of meddling discussed in the second scenario is a genuine problem for the city's welfare. The difference between these cases, or at least the difference Socrates identifies as being significant, is that in the first scenario, the meddling that occurs is between members of a single class, whereas in the second scenario, the meddling that occurs involves agents who are acting outside of their station and competence. Ultimately then, it is *inter*class meddling rather than *intra*class meddling that Socrates describes as "the worst evil one could do to [the city]" (434c).

When we turn this inward, we begin to see how Plato's notion of "inner faction" might capture something significant about the nature of ambivalence. In the case of the soul, how might these scenarios play out? Well, the first scenario seems to parallel conflicts between appetitive desires. Maybe Jack finds himself hungry but also very much hoping to catch another's eye and wanting to lose a few pounds to look good for them. Or maybe Teresa wants to have another beer and also wants to go to bed. Or maybe Marcus wants to go out with some friends while simultaneously feeling the attractions of just staying home alone.

Here it seems of relatively little importance that these appetitive conflicts have arisen. Our appetitive desires are by nature transitory: they come and go, with varying degrees of motivational force. Yet, by Plato's lights, they are normatively insignificant (in just the way you can imagine Plato regarding individual cobblers and carpenters as being politically insignificant). Whether I desire this or that, given Plato's belief that my desires systematically distort what's really of value, won't ultimately matter for the question "How should I live?" And as a result, the sort of desiderative conflict under consideration just isn't relevant to whether or not my soul is just.

On the other hand, Plato is very much concerned about *inter*part conflicts of the sort that parallel the second scenario Socrates offers to Glaucon. After all, the moneymaker who is puffed up by wealth is, in all likelihood, not just a source of injustice in his city but almost certainly the seat of an unjust soul. The rich are forever sure of their judgments about what's good or what should be done. They can't imagine that someone who has less money than they could possibly know more or be wiser. (Moreover, they do not typically restrict this judgment to the domain of their own success but imagine it to be true in any domain—see, e.g., the abject failure of successful businessmen being the general managers of the professional sports teams that they purchase.) So rather than subjecting their judgments to careful scrutiny, either by discursive engagement with others or through the laborious process of careful reflection, whatever comes to them off the cuff—thoughts conditioned on a long pattern of yes-men agreeing with his every pronouncement—shapes their behavior.

Of course, even the rich are not immune to at least momentary concerns and insecurities. And when doubt creeps in, they can experience a temporary reprieve from their ordinary state. Here it seems that some element of the rich individual's soul invites him to reconsider and to rethink the judgments that come from his over-inflated sense of self-worth. Perhaps it is the spirited element, and this takes the form of chagrin or shame. What else but shame makes sense when you appreciate, even inchoately, how your life is only possible because so many of your moral equals suffer a great deal? Or perhaps it is the man's rational element that allows him to see the folly of his actual pattern of concerns. If the moneymaker who has been puffed up by wealth confronts himself in these ways, he might simply "come to his senses," as it were, and see reason. More likely, he'll return to the familiar rationalizations that he needs to live.

Among these possibilities, the former option is of course clearly preferable, owing to the fact that only the just individual, in whose soul reasons rules, will secure *eudaimonia*. The reason for this, Plato argues, is that the latter option is inherently unstable, and so it cannot serve as a basis for the kind of long-term satisfaction and flourishing that is constitutive of the good life. As Plato tells it, a man whose soul is ordered around the love of money—a man with an *oligarchic constitution*—will eventually become more and more disordered. More base elements of the rich man's appetites, which have thus far been sublimated to his ultimate end of making money, will increase in their strength and eventually win out over the purely avaricious motives, which at least are structured around a mean conception of prudence (cf. *Republic* 557a, where Socrates discusses the transition from an oligarchy to a democracy). At that point, the rich man will be oriented toward pleasure seeking and power even though (by Socrates's lights) these pursuits are alienating, self-exhausting, and, ultimately, unsatisfying. Thus it seems that although the rich person might, upon having a moment of reflective self-awareness, fully eschew the base motives that drive him, Socrates's view is that his inner faction will ultimately push him to embrace them more fully.

Notice, however, that there is a third option here, and it's one that is actually fairly common. The minimally reflective rich man might feel quite torn or conflicted about the state of his soul. This person is certainly better off with respect to justice than his counterpart who has fully allowed his base appetitive desires to usurp his rational element. But even this is still a problem. The double-minded rich man might be able to avoid falling prey to some of his worst impulses. But so too, he is not able to fully embrace all of his best ones either, particularly those rational impulses that conflict with appetite. So while he might be more just than his fully appetitive counterpart, his soul is still dangerously unstable. After all, what we're discussing here is, in essence, a conflict at the very core of who the double-minded rich man is—between the distinct elements of his soul. In particular, it is a conflict between the rationally grounded awareness of the insignificance of wealth and a powerful appetitive thrill for it.

Now in this case we have an agent who is apparently ambivalent, but for whom we perhaps have very little sympathy otherwise. This man, we might think, should resolve his inner faction *not* necessarily because inner faction is bad as such, but because the man's love of money, which he identifies with to a great degree, is usurping reason's role in determining his priorities. And this is a problem—at least for Socrates—because reason alone can correctly apprehend the Good, at least to some approximation, while appetites like the love of money are happy to substitute true goodness with simulacra of value (517ff.). It thus seems that what really goes wrong in this sort of case of inner faction (i.e., an interpart conflict), is that at least one of the parts involved in such a conflict necessarily issues in mistaken values if it is not properly submitted to the rule of the rational element.

But before we get too far ahead of ourselves in diagnosing precisely what Plato objects to in cases of inner faction, I want to try to draw out a key lesson concerning what inner faction is and how it is (and isn't) connected to ambivalence. The main thing to notice here for our purposes is that inner faction involves conflict between the most basic elements of the human soul. Consequently, conflicts between mere appetitive desires, which are transitory and disposable, are not significant in this way. Rather, conflicts that occur between those elements of our agency that are inseparable from our practical selves are the ones that really matter. For Plato, I can be the agent I am without wanting or caring about this or that, but I cannot be who I am without the rational, spirited, and appetitive elements of my soul. Plato might of course be wrong about this—indeed, I suspect that he is—but that's not what is important here. Rather, it's that he points us toward thinking that the sense of "inner" at stake is one according to which a psychological element or state is inner if and only if it plays a necessary role in structuring the agent's practical self, such that she could not be who she is as an agent in the absence of those elements or states.

## 2.3. The Inner Self

Here Plato helps us to identify a very crucial form of practical conflict that arises between the "inner" or deepest elements of who we are. However, it is a matter of great controversy that Plato's tripartite conception of the soul correctly identifies the inner elements of our agency and their relative ordering. One might be skeptical of this for familiar Humean reasons. Perhaps we are only bundles of impressions and ideas and passions. On this "bundle theory" of the self, the very idea of an "inner self" is dubious. Alternatively, you might also be skeptical of Plato's view because you think he's either misidentified the important elements of human agency *or* misidentified their ordering.

The correct alternative to Plato's account of innermost elements human agency is a matter of some controversy among moral psychologists. Most agree with Plato in thinking that we cannot be fully identified with mere appetitive desires. The reason for this is simple: we are alienated from many of these desires—i.e., we do not regard them as "speaking" for us in an evaluatively significant way. Nor do we see them as playing a necessary role in structuring our practical selves. To see this, consider, for example, a new parent who, in the middle of another sleepless night, momentarily finds him- or herself wanting to shake the baby and then is immediately disgusted at the thought. This desire is, naturally, the new parent's in the sense that it is occurring within his or her psychology. But the immediate and powerful revulsion that the new parent experiences in the wake of the desire is revelatory: the desire in question does not in any way fit within the new parent's overall evaluative framework, within the patterns of concern that structure his or her agency. The possibility of this degree of alienation shows that the desire in question was merely lurking at the very periphery of the new parent's practical self. It was, we might say, no more than a causal force that he or she experienced and not a motive the new parent was prepared to license as authoritative for her in the moment or in any close alternative possibilities.

But if this desire is at the very edges of agency—so far from the new parent's practical identity that it does not speak to who he or she is—many other desires are much closer. These are desires that we might want to dissociate from, at least in some contexts, even while embracing them in others. I suspect that desires for *stuff*—desires for a new iPhone or a new pair of (unnecessary) shoes, or a Martin D28—are often like this. Indeed I often find myself in the grips of such a desire, wanting, for example, a D28 while *simultaneously* being deeply suspicious of that motive, since it is very plausibly the product of external, corporate influences that I do not regard as good.

These sorts of cases teach us two important things. First, they show that even if mere desires do not constitute our innermost selves, they are not all so far removed from the most central elements of our practical identities as is the desire to shake the child. My desire for the new Martin is not something that repulses me, but neither is it something is I am fully behind, in part because I am suspicious of its genealogy. Yet suspicions or no, if I were to buy a Martin D28, it wouldn't be an accident, nor would it look like a fully alien force animating my behavior. It'd be *my* action in a meaningful sense. On the other hand, if I never act on this desire, I would do nothing out of character. Indeed, if the desire disappears from my psychology altogether, such that I never even have another yen for an expensive guitar, my practical self is all but unchanged. This points us toward a second lesson. It seems that part of what explains why desires—even ones that we identify with to some degree—are not necessarily part of our deep or inner selves is that we can excise them from our motivational set without doing substantial violence to our practical identities.

The elements of our *inner* selves therefore seem to have at least two key properties that are missing in the case of mere desires. First, we must be able to identify with the attitude in question or stand behind it to a significant degree. This won't entail that we never feel alienated from that motivational impulse, but it does mean that in a wide range of circumstances, we regard it as having some authority to move us to action.[9] Second, the elements or states in question must be such that if we were to lose them, we would thereby radically alter our practical identities. There are thus a subjective component and an objective component to innerness.

But if mere desires lack one or both of these properties (and so cannot constitute our deepest selves), what psychological states or dispositions could do this? For Plato, motives issuing from one's rational element are certainly inner. But in the intervening twenty-three hundred years, many philosophers have come to think that this is only one possible account of the extension of inner psychological states. In fact, in response to just this question, moral psychologists have supplied an impressive list of alternative psychological states that might do the job. It has been suggested inter alia that the deepest elements of our agency—the ones necessarily implicated in cases of inner faction—are reflexive, higher-order desires (Frankfurt 1971), what we care about (Frankfurt 1988;

---

[9] There is a strand of argument, developed most clearly by J. David Velleman (1992), that moves directly from the fact that we can be alienated from a state or class of states to the conclusion that that state or class of states cannot be identified with the agent. This inference seems too strong, owing to the fact that I can be alienated from, say, a friend without that feeling of alienation fully severing the friendship. So too, I submit, I can be alienated from my desire to buy the Martin D28 to *some* degree without being fully alienated from it, so it is still a desire that is "my own" in at least an attenuated sense.

Shoemaker 2003; and Jaworska 2007), what we take to be valuable (Watson 1975 and Korsgaard 1986), what we value (Watson 1987 and Scheffler 2011), or what we love (Frankfurt 2004).

These views are typically framed as competitors, but I confess to doubting that there is a single class of psychological attitudes that uniquely meets the two conditions on innerness. Insofar as we can perspicuously distinguish between the attitudes in question, I readily identify with instances of each of these. My reflexive higher-order volition that my desire to get some work done this afternoon be the one that moves me to action is one that I recognize as my own. So too, the care and concern I have for the success of a particular American football team (the currently execrable Carolina Panthers) is something that I identify with. I also see my judgment that it's important not to cross picket lines as really being my own. This is true as well for my valuing of time spent outside with friends (and maybe with a cold beer in hand). And while I do not think that I *am* what I love, as some have suggested, I think the distance between who I am most fundamentally and what I love, particularly the love I feel for my wife, our daughters, and our life together, is vanishingly small. I thus *identify* my agency with instances of each of these states.[10] Consequently, I think that these classes of psychological attitudes all meet the subjective criterion on being part of my inner self.

Let's turn now to the question of the role that attitudes of these sorts play in shaping who I am as an agent. In order for them to count as inner, I have suggested not only that I must endorse or associate myself with the psychological states in question, but also

---

[10] Of course despite this, I can, as an intellectual exercise, follow Thomas Nagel's (1971) lead and notice that my reflexive higher-order desires, cares, judgments of value, valuings, and loves are all contingent, and that the seriousness with which I engage the objects of these attitudes is absurd (as Nagel understands it). But even if this shows that I can be alienated from these attitudes in the sense that it is possible for me to no longer regard them as rationally *necessary*, it does not follow that I can be alienated from these states *tout court*.

that they must be such that were I to dissociate myself from them, I would do significant violence to my practical identity as it now exists. This test very clearly introduces a scalar element to the property of innerness. After all, I would do more violence to who I am as an agent if I were to dissociate myself from my love for my family than I would if I were to dissociate myself from the concern I have for how the Panthers are doing. However, the fact that I would do more damage to my practical identity by dissociating from the people I love doesn't mean that my fandom for a particular football team isn't part of my inner self. In fact, if I had to distance myself from *any* of the kinds of attitudes under consideration, it would require alterations to my practical self that stand in stark contrast to those that would occur if I dissociated myself from a mere desire for a fancy new guitar or from a preference for desserts that are savory rather than (exclusively) sweet. To no longer regard one of these relatively trivial desires as authoritative does nothing to my agency, or so little that it isn't worth mentioning. It seems, then, that my cares, values, and loves can each meet the objective criterion on being part of my inner self, while more superficial, transient motives do not.

Owing to the fact that the inner self is the site of inner faction, it seems to follow that if ambivalence is to be a kind of inner faction, it cannot involve conflicts between motives or attitudes that the agent doesn't identify herself with or that are such that were she to dissociate herself from them, it would be of little consequence for her practical self.[11] As a result, ambivalence seems to require that an

---

[11] In narrowing the scope of my account of ambivalence to *inner* faction, I am circumscribing the concept in a way that might miss some elements of our experiences with ambivalence broadly understood. In the spirit of taking the full range of experiences that we are sometimes tempted to call "ambivalence," Hili Razinsky (2017) argues that ambivalence should be defined as follows:

> A person is ambivalent . . . if she holds two opposed mental attitudes toward one and the same object. The attitudes must be opposed in their capacity as that person's attitudes. Less formally, they have to be opposed in the sense that implies they are opposed from the point of view of the ambivalent

agent experience a conflict between inter alia what she cares about, values, or loves. And this is precisely what we see in Erica's and Dimmesdale's cases. It isn't a conflict between fleeting desires that tears them apart. It is instead an inherent tension between some of their deepest commitments and values. And this is precisely why we experience ambivalence as a problem: to resolve the conflict, it seems like we will have to betray ourselves.

Of course, this can't be *all* there is to ambivalence. After all, the conflict that arises for me when a Panthers game is on at the same time that I need to take my daughter to a close friend's birthday party is not one that I experience as an instance of ambivalence. Yet it is by hypothesis an instance of inner faction insofar as it involves two of the attitudes that constitute who I am as an agent. Accordingly, we need to say more about the precise nature of ambivalence to better identify the exact kind of inner faction that it really is.

person. A person is ambivalent according to this definition who, for example, wants to change her life, and yet at the same time does not want to change it, or again, who judges an acquaintance kind and also, ambivalently, judges the acquaintance unkind. (Razinsky 2017, 16)

This account clearly includes forms of mental opposition that I want to exclude from my analysis. For example, Razinsky understands opposing judgments or beliefs to be instances of ambivalence, whereas I think that any opposition that occurs between our beliefs does so largely outside of the realm of human agency. This means that the object of Razinsky's analysis is not a wholly practical matter. Yet as I see it, ambivalence, at its core, is something that occurs because we are the kind of agents who care, value, and love.

Of course, the breadth of Razinsky's analysis doesn't make it inferior to the one I offer here, though it does mean that what Razinsky and I are up to is subtly but importantly different. An important advantage to Razinsky's approach is that it accommodates features of ordinary language and experience that mine leaves out—we do, in fact, describe ourselves as being ambivalent about what to order at a restaurant or about what to believe. On the other hand, an important reason why I am interested in a more narrowly circumscribed phenomenon is that it lines up more closely with the variety of ambivalence that unificationists going back to Plato have been keen to reject. Despite these differences, however, Razinsky, along with Wolf (2002), Poltera (2011), and Gunnarsson (2014), is correctly worried that attempts at dismissing ambivalence are missing something deeply important about what it means to be a well-functioning human person.

## 2.4. Ambivalence as *Necessary* Inner Faction

Harry Frankfurt, who is largely responsible for reviving interest in the subject of ambivalence among contemporary analytic philosophers, posits two conditions on ambivalence.

> Ambivalence is constituted by conflicting volitional movements or tendencies, either conscious or unconscious, that meet two conditions. First, they are inherently and hence unavoidably opposed; that is, they do not just happen to conflict on account of contingent circumstances. Second, they are both wholly internal to a person's will rather than alien to him; that is, he is not passive with respect to them. An example of ambivalence might be provided by someone who is moved to commit himself to a certain career, or to a certain person, and also moved to refrain from doing so. (Frankfurt 1992, 8)

As we see with the second condition, Frankfurt's view follows the Platonic tradition of holding that ambivalence is a distinctive because it involves a division in the inner elements of our practical selves. This account therefore rules out conflicts of the sort one faces when confronted by a dessert menu filled with many tempting options as being instances of ambivalence. Only conflicts that occur between those elements of our practical selves that compose the core of who we are as agents can be regarded as instances of ambivalence.

But Frankfurt doesn't limit his account of ambivalence to inner faction. He insists, first, that in addition to involving inner faction, the conflict between the elements of the agent's will must be *necessary*—"unavoidably opposed." This sort of opposition occurs, for example, when you find yourself loving someone and also find yourself quite opposed to the person and to this love. Here we might think again of Arthur Dimmesdale, who, late in the novel confirms his continued love for Hester, but who also is deeply opposed to that part of his practical identity.

As stated, this is a very restrictive account of ambivalence, at least when we read Frankfurt in an overly wooden way. For example, on Frankfurt's account, it at least appears as if Erica cannot be ambivalent about whether to take the new job or stay close to her parents. After all, her conflict is clearly "contingent" in some sense. If she had more money in her bank account, she could just invite her parents to relocate with her. If the opportunity didn't require her to move, then she could take it without it affecting her ability to care for family. These facts demonstrate that the motives animating Erica's inner tension are not necessarily opposed in the way Frankfurt seems to require.

Understood this way, it seems that Frankfurt's is much too strict a requirement. Why should the fact that Erica's inner faction involves volitional movements or tendencies that are only contingently opposed mean that she is not ambivalent? Why isn't the fact that they are *actually* opposed enough?

One way to address this is to simply insist that Erica is in fact ambivalent, and conclude on that basis that ambivalence doesn't require necessary opposition, treating paradigm cases such as hers as a backstop in our theorizing. This is tempting. After all, as a general methodological presumption, when theorizing about complex phenomena such as ambivalence, we do well not to imperiously demarcate overly fixed boundaries—particularly ones that seem opposed to common experience. When we fail to do this and instead hope to gain precision or clarity by ex ante proscriptions on what is and what isn't within the purview of a theory of something like ambivalence, we often miss some of the richness of the phenomenon and its importance to human lives, which was surely part of what spurred our philosophical reflection in the first place.

But though I think it is possible to read Frankfurt here as being overly narrow in his diagnosis of ambivalence, I do not think his first requirement on ambivalence actually commits him to ruling out ambivalence in cases like Erica's. Consider, for example, the experience from Erica's point of view. She very much identifies with her career ambitions—she *cares* about them or *values* them, to put the point in terms of those volitional elements that constitute her inner self. But she also very much identifies with her parents and with her continued role as their caregiver. She *loves* them as well. Now, when you care about something, that element of your psychology issues in specific desires—desires that enjoin you to promote that thing, or to honor or respect it, or to enjoy it. This is also true of what you value and love. In fact, any of the elements that constitute our inner selves do so in part in virtue of the first-order motivations that they issue in—the motivations that directly move us to action. Indeed, it is through these desires that our cares, values, and loves robustly structure our behavior across a wide range of alternative possibilities. Accordingly, we should consider *these* direct motivations to be "inner," since, when they issue from our inner selves, they've inherited the action-guiding authority of their sources.

In Erica's case, it's surely true that the value she attaches to her career ambitions issues in desires to accept the job offer, move to a new town, make arrangements for someone else to care for her parents, etc. It's also surely true that the love she has for her parents and for the specifics of their relationship leads her to feel repulsed by the idea of taking the job or moving and horrified at the thought of someone else caring for them during their last years. And these feelings are no doubt connected to first-order motives to stay in her current job and town and to keep caring for her folks.

Here we can see how even in Erica's practical conflict, there is necessary conflict between elements of her inner self. She has both desires to take the job, move, and leave her parents in the care of someone else and desires that none of these come to pass. That she has these opposing desires is, of course, due to contingent circumstances—she might be unconcerned about her career or about caregiving—but the opposition of these desires is not contingent. No matter the circumstances, if you have a desire to $x$ and either a desire to $\sim x$ or a desire that $x$ not obtain, your desires are in opposition to one another. And because in cases like Erica's the opposing desires are each connected in a direct way to her inner self, the necessary opposition counts as a case of *inner* faction. Perhaps this isn't quite what Frankfurt has in mind when he claims that the "volitional movements or tendencies" that compose the agent's inner self must be "inherently and hence unavoidably opposed" (1992, 8). But if he is indeed correct in thinking that there must be some form of necessary opposition between an agent's inner elements in order for that agent to be ambivalent, the kind of opposition sketched here suffices.

## 2.5.  A Further Constraint

However, even allowing that Frankfurt is correct in thinking that ambivalence is a form of necessary inner faction, there is more to be said about the nature of ambivalence. In particular, I want to suggest that there is a reflexive element inherent to ambivalence, which concerns the ambivalent agent's "take" on her dilemma. She must, I submit, regard her conflict as being one that cannot be resolved without significant *value remainder* or *value residue*. That is, she must have some conception of her conflict as being one that, no matter how she proceeds, there will be some significant value "left on the table" that cannot reasonably be ignored.

It's for this reason that I do not regard the inner conflict that arises between my sports fandom and the birthday party I've promised to take my daughter to as really being an instance of ambivalence. It's true of course, that my attitudes toward various sports teams are part of my inner self. In the case of the Panthers, for example, I try to watch all of their games. I read about the team, and try to understand the offensive and defensive schemes that they're running so that I can better appreciate them. I get happy when they win and sad when they lose. Etc., etc., etc. For all that, my love for my daughter and my concern to support her projects—even ones that I don't care about independently of her interests—is even more central to who I am as an agent. Yet because these inner elements issue in necessarily opposed desires (wanting to be at park at 3:00 p.m. on Sunday and not wanting to be at the park at 3:00 p.m. on Sunday), the conflict that arises between these two elements is necessary inner faction.

However, in this case, I do not regard missing the game as being a *significant* cost that's left over from my choice to attend the game. In cases of value remainder, after all, the residual value of the choice that is not pursued will typically invite us to take certain retrospective attitudes toward the choice itself. We regret that we had to do it. Or we lament or mourn, or grieve the loss of unrealized value. But I do not regard the disvalue of missing this week's game (which, let's be honest, they were probably going to lose anyway), as something to regret or lament or mourn or grieve. Of course, I do betray some element of who I am, but the "betrayal," such as it is, has its source not in some alien force moving me contrary to my will, but in one of the deepest elements of who I am as an agent—my love for my daughter.

Clearly, this is very different from the case of necessary inner faction that Erica experiences. In her case, she is devoted to both her parents and her own ambitions, and she recognizes that, given her situation, there is no way to resolve the conflict that has arisen between these concerns without missing out on something she cares about greatly. In other words, Erica quite reasonably feels as if she can't avoid doing damage to her practical self. After all, she reasons, the realization of either of her options will meaningfully preclude the realization of some other commitment or value that heretofore has defined her—she senses that "she can't have it all." But this just another way of saying that she clearly regards the choice as being one in which there is significant value remainder. Of course, she will probably not conceive of it in those terms, but her longing to *per impossible* pursue each option reveals that she is sensitive to the fact that no way of resolving her dilemma will be free from significant cost. The stark difference between Erica's conflict and my own suggests that necessary inner faction is not sufficient for ambivalence. Ambivalent agents face necessary inner factions that they regard themselves as not being able to resolve without significant remainder.

## 2.6. Two Ways to Be Ambivalent

At this point, I think we've got a more or less workable account of what ambivalence is. But before turning to the question whether ambivalence as such is an agential failing, I want to consider one final distinction we can make about ambivalence. This distinction is also due to Harry Frankfurt (1988), and it concerns the precise nature of conflicts that arise between inner motives. According to Frankfurt, there are two kinds of conflicts that occur within an ambivalent will:

> In conflicts of the one sort, [inner motives] compete for priority or position in a preferential order; the issue is which [inner motive] to satisfy *first*. In conflicts of the other sort, the issue is whether a [inner motive] should be given *any* place in the order of preference at all—that is, whether it is to be endorsed as a legitimate candidate for satisfaction or whether it is to be rejected as entitled to no priority whatsoever. When a conflict of the first kind is resolved, the competing [inner motives] are *integrated* into a single ordering, within which each occupies a specific position. Resolving a conflict of the second kind involves radical *separation* of the competing [inner motives], one of which is not merely assigned a relatively less favored position but extruded entirely as an outlaw. (1988, 170)

This distinction roughly tracks differences in the varieties of ambivalence that Erica and Dimmesdale experience respectively. For Erica, the problem is that her new career opportunity forces her into a conflict between inner elements that henceforth have not needed to be ordered. Her ambivalence, in other words, is one that concerns whether to prioritize her career over family or to prioritize family over career. In Dimmesdale's case, at least as he conceptualizes it, he does not think the pull of God's commands on the one hand and his feelings for Hester that "had a consecration of [their] own" (152) on the other can simultaneously coexist in his innermost self. The tension and anxiety he feels therefore owes to the fact that he believes that one of these motives must be "extruded entirely as an outlaw" (Frankfurt 1988, 170).

Following J. S. Swindell (2010), I think that it's helpful to sort the two types of conflicts that Frankfurt identifies here into conflicts of "willing" and "identifying" respectively.[12] Conflicts of the former sort are, I suspect, more familiar. We are often conflicted about how we should order those inner motives that we identify with. Consider Neal, who identifies with his concern to be a good teacher for his students, but who also identifies with his abiding concern to be a good partner, friend, and parent. Each of these makes considerable claims on his time. How should he balance them? Like many of us in similar situations, he's not always sure, and as a result, Neal sometimes find himself ambivalent about what to do in cases in which these two elements of who he is are pitted against one another. But though this kind of ambivalence can be psychically distressing, according to Frankfurt, we can resolve ambivalence of this sort simply by "integrating" the inner motives we identify with into a single commensurate list that provides a determinate ranking of priorities.

---

[12] J. S. Swindell (2010) develops this point on the way to developing a full taxonomy of ambivalence.

The second kind of conflict that Frankfurt discusses is perhaps less common than the first (though it is still familiar enough). It involves being divided over whether some volitional element can really continue to be *one's own* or whether that motive should instead be wholly rejected as alien. Here the issue isn't one of balancing or "ordering" competing motivations. Instead it's a matter of whether one (or more) of the competing motives can continue to be counted as "inner" in the relevant sense. Dimmesdale experiences this kind of conflict. But although his is a rather heightened example of a conflict of identifying, it's not completely unique. After all, the questions of whether to continue a relationship or not, or of whether you really love a person or not, are familiar enough, even if one is confronted with these conflicts for earthly reasons rather than divine. But in either case, it's doubtful these conflicting movements can be integrated into a single ordering. It seems, then, that to resolve ambivalence of this sort an agent must "outlaw" one of the motives entirely, which for Frankfurt involves giving it *no* place in one's deliberative economy. In other words, to resolve conflicts of identifying, one must fully identify with one inner motive and exile the other from one's inner self.

It is in precisely these cases that we feel most clearly that however we choose, there will be significant value remainder. When, in an effort to resolve our ambivalence, we outlaw one of our inner motives, we cut ourselves off from something that has mattered significantly to us and that we regarded as being a real source of value. And I suspect that it is *this* feature of ambivalence (at least in conflicts of identifying), even more than the internal tension itself, that upsets us so greatly when we are faced with significant practical dilemmas. This loss is also present, though in an attenuated form if we resolve conflicts of willing in the way Frankfurt prescribes. Until the new job offer came, Erica was able to treat her career ambitions and love for her parents as equally central to her life prospects. But in its wake, she has to consciously decide how to prioritize these two things. And this brings into sharp relief what's lost by choosing one determinate ranking over the other.

Frankfurt's keen observation that ambivalent agents can be divided in at least two ways means that the general phenomenon of ambivalence cannot be neatly reduced to a single form of conflict. All ambivalence might be, as I have been suggesting, necessary inner faction that is experienced as irresolvable without value remainder, but this account sensibly leaves leeway for multiple forms that that inner faction might take. Indeed, this reflects the variation of feelings that we describe as ambivalence—the tension that the minimally reflective rich person feels when he confronts his love for money but is not prepared to eschew it fully, the sense of self-betrayal that worries Erica when she considers her options, and the longing for freedom that animates Paul's frustrations with his all too human motivations.

## 2.7. Conclusion

The account of ambivalence I've developed in this chapter is, I hope, sufficiently attentive to the phenomenon itself. That is, I have tried to make sure that my theorizing does not stray too far from the concerns that lead us to experience ambivalence as psychically taxing. In so doing, I've taken pains to connect the experience of ambivalence as I understand it to the phenomenon that exercised Plato, Saints Paul and Augustine, and more recently, unificationists like Harry Frankfurt.[13] Hopefully, I've succeeded in this aim, since the rest of the book is devoted, first, to explaining

---

[13] Alexander Jech (2013) argues that although Augustine's and Kierkegaard's proposed analyses of wholeheartedness are importantly different from the account proposed by Frankfurt, all three are worried about the same purported malady. This suggests that although the historical antecedents to Frankfurt's view weren't always careful to specify what precisely ambivalence involves (Kierkegaard is a notable exception in this regard), they were meaning to pick out the same thing.

why unificationists are mistaken when they argue that ambivalence so understood is necessarily an agential failing and, second, to arguing that ideal agency actually requires us to be open to the forms of ambivalence discussed here. Ambivalence need not be the result of a disordered will. Instead, it can be, and very often is, the very thing that signifies a well-functioning one.

# 3
# Resolving the Will

## 3.1. Three Unificationist Arguments

There are three key arguments in the unificationist tradition: the *Resolution Argument*, the *Affirmation Argument*, and the master argument, the *Argument from Self-Defeat*. These arguments each purport to show that an ambivalent agent is missing something absolutely crucial for ideal or well-functioning agency. By contrast, the properties identified by unificationists advancing these arguments—autonomy, meaning, and integrity respectively—are all possessed by the unified or wholehearted agent, who has mastered her inner faction, either by creating a determinate ordering of priorities (in the case of conflicts of willing) or by wholly extruding recalcitrant motives from her inner self (in the case of conflicts of identifying). Well-functioning agency is thus to be identified with unified or wholehearted agency.

In the next four chapters, however, I want to upset this general argumentative strategy by showing that ambivalence as such is not at odds with the valuable properties unificationists seek to preserve. First, I'll argue (in this chapter) that ambivalent agents can resolve their wills without fully and unequivocally standing behind one of the opposing motives over the other. As a result, even ambivalent agents can be autonomous agents rather than passive vehicles for desiderative forces. So too (I argue in Chapter 4), ambivalent agents can affirm their choices in meaning-grounding ways even if they cannot univocally stand behind them in the way that wholehearted agents can. In fact, we'll see that ambivalence can enhance rather than detract from the significance of an agent's affirmation. Finally

*In Praise of Ambivalence*. D. Justin Coates, Oxford University Press. © Oxford University Press 2023.
DOI: 10.1093/oso/9780197652398.003.0003

I'll argue (in Chapters 5 and 6) that insofar as agential integrity is valuable for its own sake, it is ambivalence and not wholeheartedness that can best secure it in a wide range of familiar cases.

With the "big picture" overview out of the way, I now turn to the first of these unificationist arguments: the Resolution Argument.

## 3.2. The Resolution Argument

The Resolution Argument is an attempt to spell out the thought that an agent who faces a dilemma and is ambivalent does not (and perhaps cannot) really resolve her will in a way that is fully *autonomous* or *self-governed*. The reason for this is that by maintaining her ambivalence in the face of a difficult practical conflict, the agent does not settle her will, and so her movements are not really *hers*, since it is not due to *her own* reflective endorsement of one motive over the other that she is moved to act. Rather, she is merely caused to do something by a motive that she does not contrastively endorse. This means that the ambivalent agent is, in a word, passive with respect to the question of how to resolve her will, and so the mere fact that she causes some state of affairs does not reflect her agency in the way that self-governed actions reflect the self that governs them.

Christine M. Korsgaard expresses just this thought:

> In order to be autonomous, it is essential that your movements be caused by you, by you operating as a unit, not by some force that is working in you or on you. So, in order to be an agent, you need to be unified—you need to put your *whole self*, so to speak, behind your movements. . . . Otherwise, you are just a mere heap of impulses, and not an agent after all. (2009, 213; emphasis added)

Here we see Korsgaard moving stepwise from claims about what's required for autonomy to a conclusion that entails that the movements of an ambivalent agent—one who acts or, if Korsgaard is correct, merely appears to act—cannot really be autonomous because they are not the agent's.

Harry Frankfurt (2004), taking up a similar strand of argument, starts with the claim that when we are ambivalent, our wills are indeterminate. What he means by this is that in cases of ambivalence, there is no fact of the matter as to which motive *we*, the agent, stand behind. Accordingly, he thinks that neither of the motives that are present in the case of ambivalence "speaks for" the person, since in the absence of the agent resolving ambivalence by endorsing one of the motives in question, the agent has not "become *finally and unequivocally clear* as to which side of the conflict he is on" (Frankfurt 2004, 91; emphasis added). Yet without this kind of resolution, the agent herself is not governing her behavior but simply is being pushed by whichever motive proves strongest.

Of course, this isn't to say that the effective motive would be moving this agent in the exact same way that a completely alien force does (for example, the way an unwilling addict's desires move him or the way a kleptomaniac's desires move her). But like a movement caused by an alien force, because the effective motive is in opposition with another inner motive and no authoritative verdict has been rendered decisively in its favor, it cannot be fully hers. Moreover, the actions of an ambivalent person are similar to those caused by alien forces in another way. Such forces can cause my movements, but they cannot rationalize them. Nor can they provide me with reasons to continue taking the means to the ends to which I am being driven. Similarly, without decisive resolution on the part of the agent, the fact that one inner motive happens to be effective rather than its contrary doesn't seem relevant when assessing the question of which motive should guide and structure our behavior prospectively and how it should do so. As Frankfurt puts it, such a motive would, like its alien counterpart, lack "guiding authority" (2004, 92).

Behind these ruminations, I think that we can tease out an interesting and powerful argument. As I understand it, this argument can be reconstructed as follows.

The Resolution Argument

(1) An agent acts autonomously only if the motive that causes her to act is "her own."

(2) A motive is the agent's own only if she unifies herself behind it or "finally and unequivocally" stands behind that motive.

(3) An agent unifies herself / fully stands behind the motive that causes her movements only if she has decisively resolved that *that* motive be the cause of her movements.

(4) When an agent is ambivalent, she has not decisively resolved the question of which motive should cause her movements.

(5) Therefore, if the agent acts without first dissolving her ambivalence, she is necessarily caused to do so by a motive that she is not unified behind / does not stand behind.

(6) Therefore, the motive that causes the ambivalent agent to act is not her own.

(7) Therefore, the ambivalent agent does not act autonomously.

From this, it seems to follow fairly straightforwardly that ambivalence as such is a threat to well-functioning agency. After all, the well-functioning agent is presumably an autonomous one. So if ambivalence rules out autonomy then it seems to simply follow that the ambivalent agent is not well functioning. Accordingly, because ambivalence undermines our ability to be unified behind / fully stand behind our actions, it renders us, if not "not an agent after all," as Korsgaard suggests, a sorely deficient agent at best.

To evaluate the soundness of this argument, we'll need to consider its crucial premise: that a motive is the agent's own only if she has decisively resolved to unify herself behind / fully stand behind that motive. I'll argue that this is false. It is in fact possible to stand behind a motive in a way that renders it your own even if you have not decisively resolved to unequivocally stand behind it. Consequently, the Resolution Argument gives us no compelling reason to think that ambivalence precludes autonomy or renders you a deficient agent in any way.

## 3.3. Resolution and Authority

In Chapter 2, when we were unpacking the precise nature of ambivalence, we saw two types of conflicts that can occur: conflicts of willing and conflicts of identifying. According to Frankfurt (and Swindell 2010), these two forms of inner conflict are distinguished according to the type of *resolution* that the conflict in question calls for. Recall that in conflicts of willing, resolution requires that we be able to integrate the conflicting motives or values in a single determinate ordering. A failure to do this, it seems, would entail a failure to fully achieve resolution. And that, the unificationists claim, means that whichever motive it is that causes your action won't be one you unequivocally stand behind, and so it is not really *your* motive.

In conflicts of identifying, resolution requires that we are able to extrude or "outlaw" (at least) one of the conflicting motives or values entirely from our practical identity. Frankfurt expands on what this means:

> In order for a conflict . . . to be resolved, so that the person is freed of his ambivalence, it is not necessary that either of his conflicting impulses disappear. It is not even necessary that either of them increase or diminish in strength. *Resolution requires only that the person become finally and unequivocally clear as to which side of the conflict he is on.* The forces mobilized on the other side may then persist with as much intensity as before; but as soon

as he has definitely established just where he himself stands, his will is no longer divided and his ambivalence is therefore gone. He has placed himself wholeheartedly behind one of the conflicting impulses, and not at all behind the other. (2004, 91; emphasis added)

Here Frankfurt is clear in stating that whatever extrusion or outlawing a motive comes to, it does not mean that you eliminate its causal force. After all, that is not something that is within the scope of our volitional powers. We cannot make the motivational "oomph" of a desire (or evaluative judgment, or concern for, or love of, or . . .) go away directly by an act of will. However deciding to regard that motive as having no normative significance for us (or "guiding authority," as Frankfurt puts it elsewhere) is within the scope of our volitional powers. So when Frankfurt claims that an agent resolves herself in conflicts of identifying by outlawing one of the conflicting impulses, he's not making a claim about the agent's *motivational* profile. Instead, he's making a claim about the agent coming to see one of the motives as being exclusively *authoritative*.

Frankfurt goes on to contrast ambivalence with *wholeheartedness* and relies on this distinction to help explain why resolution is impossible for an ambivalent agent.

If ambivalence is a disease of the mind, the health of the mind requires a unified will. That is, the mind is healthy—at least with respect to its volitional faculty—insofar as it is wholehearted. Being wholehearted means having a will that is undivided. The wholehearted person is fully settled as to what he wants, and what he cares about. With regard to any conflict of dispositions or inclinations within himself, he has no doubts or reservations as to where he stands. He lends himself to his caring and loving unequivocally and without reserve. Thus his identification with the volitional configurations that define his final ends is neither inhibited nor qualified. (2004, 95)

According to Frankfurt, being wholehearted entails that an agent's will is structured in a way such that it is unequivocally clear as to which motive the agent identifies herself with. And as we just saw, this unequivocal clarity has important implications: to be whole-hearted about a motive is to be "behind" it fully and not at all "be-hind" conflicting motives. And as a result, when we wholeheartedly endorse one motive over another, it seems that we become ration-ally committed to the endorsed motive and rationally alienated from the unendorsed motives. How could I, after all, be rational in acting on a motive at I am in no way behind?

It therefore seems that only a wholehearted endorsement of one of the conflicting motives resolves an agent's ambivalence because it renders the unendorsed motive rationally inconsequential for the agent. Accordingly, for Frankfurt, wholehearted endorsement of one motivational tendency over another is action-guiding, since wholehearted endorsements provide us with *reason* to pursue the former course of action and, upon our pursuing that course of ac-tion, it *speaks for us*—it is *our own*. Wholeheartedness, being undi-vided, or, to return to Korsgaard's characterization of the form of endorsement in question, "putting your whole self . . . behind your movements," is therefore the basis for autonomous agency, which is perhaps the ideal for which all well-functioning agents strive.

Unfortunately, none of this is possible when we are ambivalent, since in cases of ambivalence the question of which motive *should* move me to action is still unsettled, even if, because I have been forced to choose, one of the motives has moved me. When an am-bivalent agent acts, it seems that the motive that is causing her to act is effective solely because of the strength of its motivational force and not at all because it has inherited the normative authority to speak for the agent. Actions issuing from an ambivalent will thus appear to be simply the output of a causal process that occurs within the agent and not genuine exercises of rational agency it-self. Indeed, this is precisely what Korsgaard is getting at when she concludes that if you are not fully behind the motive that animates your movements, "you are just a mere heap of impulses, and not an agent after all" (2009, 213).

## 3.4. An Anti-unificationist Alternative?

The key problem with this argument is that it's far from clear that the *rational* or *authoritative* resolution requires that the agent wholeheartedly endorse a single ordering of motives (in conflicts of willing) or one option over another, or one motive over another (in conflicts of identifying), such that the unendorsed motive is regarded as wholly lacking action-guiding authority for her. Indeed, we might reasonably ask: why isn't it possible to resolve ourselves simply by determining what it is that we have most reason to care about or what it is that we have most reason to do, and then go from there? No doubt, this will not completely solve the psychic distress of being of two minds, but as Frankfurt himself admits, even a wholehearted endorsement of one course of action over another will not necessarily diminish the conflicting constituents of our psychologies. So again, couldn't a less-than-wholehearted choice, when consciously made for reasons, rationally commit us to the projects that follow from our decisions and so rationally resolve the question of what to do?

Frankfurt thinks not. This is because, on his view, such an arrangement would be inherently unstable, and as a result, it could not resolve our ambivalence at a fundamental level. In particular, he claims:

> [When an agent] cannot bring himself to identify decisively either with one of the opposing tendencies of will or the other . . . [that agent] is volitionally fragmented. His will is unstable and incoherent, moving him in contrary directions simultaneously or in a disorderly sequence. He suffers from a radically entrenched ambivalence, in which his will remains obstinately undefined and

therefore lacks *effective guiding authority*. As long as he is unable to resolve the conflict by which he is torn, and thus to unify his will, the person is at odds with himself.

Suppose, for example, that he is ambivalent with respect to loving a certain woman. Part of him loves her, but part of him is opposed to loving her; and he himself is undecided concerning which of his two inconsistent tendencies he wants to prevail. . . . Since he is unresolved whether to support his love of the woman, or to identify himself with and to mobilize his energies behind his opposition to that love, he is unresolved as to whether he does truly love her. Thus his will is indeterminate. (Frankfurt 2004, 92–93; emphasis added)

For Frankfurt, then, it's not enough that an agent makes a choice concerning two inconsistent tendencies. If that choice does not issue from a motive that has been wholeheartedly endorsed, then any apparent resolution that it comes from the agent regarding one motive as being preferable, at least to some degree in the present circumstances, is ultimately illusory.

The underlying argument Frankfurt has in mind here is something like the following. Suppose that I am ambivalent with respect to the question of whether or not to $x$, and I decide to $x$. But further suppose that I do so not because I wholeheartedly endorse $x$-ing but because I must simply make a decision one way or the other, and in the circumstances, I come to believe that $x$-ing has some things going for it, say that it would be pleasurable or that it would be soothing. In this case, you might think that the mere fact that I chose $x$ for these reasons does nothing to stop me from reflectively doubting the legitimacy of my decision to $x$. In such a case, I could always wonder, "Well sure, I guess this will feel nice, but is it really what I want to be doing now?" In so doing, I am questioning the authority of that decision made for that reason to guide my behavior going forward. And because the ability to reflectively question the legitimacy of a motive or plan of action is, for Frankfurt, the sine qua non of a motive or plan of action that an agent can be alienated from, such motives or plans of action cannot *be the agent's own.* Yet if the motive that moves me to action is not my own (in the relevant sense of "my own"), then it is hard to see how I am thereby rationally committed to taking the means to that end. How could that motive rationally and effectively guide my projects or how I conceive of my life more generally? Presumably, it cannot. As a consequence, Frankfurt concludes that even decisions made for reasons cannot resonate in the agent's practical identity in an authoritatively action-guiding way when those decisions issue from an indeterminate or ambivalent will.

### 3.5. Agency and Normative Competence

Though this is a rhetorically powerful rejoinder to the idea that rational resolution—i.e., resolving one's will done on the basis of reasons—is sufficient to account for why the decisions made by ambivalent agents can be their own and so self-governed, I do not think that it ultimately succeeds. The reason for this, we'll see, is that when we decide to act for reasons, we are exercising our normative competence. And this alone is sufficient for the action being *your* action in the sense at stake for autonomy, even in cases in which you do not fully stand behind your action in the way required for unity and wholeheartedness.

But in order to show that an action can be your own even if you do not fully stand behind it, I will begin in a somewhat surprising place by considering the normative significance of cases of promissory obligation. Let's think, then, of a case in which when you make a promise to a friend, say to help him move. Ordinarily, when you make a promise, you are thereby committed to taking the necessary means to keeping that promise. This means, for example, that if you agreed to start helping him at 9:00 a.m. and it takes fifteen minutes to get to your friend's house, then ordinarily you'll have decisive reason to leave your house by 8:45 a.m. The explanation for why this reason should exist and have this degree of weightiness is obvious: promises have action-guiding authority such that in unexceptional circumstances, they are sufficient to fully resolve the question of what to do.

Of course if you make a promise under duress or because another agent has threatened you, then the promise itself fails to provide you with reason to comply. Your promise and the circumstances of you making it aren't typical, and so it is not binding in the way we ordinarily think of promises as being binding. In addition to conditions like duress and coercion, which excuse one from promissory obligations, agents who fail to comprehend the weightiness of promissory obligation (e.g., young children), agents who are not of "sound mind," and agents who have been misled as to the true nature of what they're agreeing to in making the promise, all seem to be excused from promissory obligation as well.

However, unlike duress or coercion, or indeed any of the other conditions on promissory obligation, being ambivalent about what one promises doesn't seem to undermine the rational weightiness or action-guiding authority of the promise itself. In other words, the mere fact that you experience inner conflict at the time of the promise doesn't mean that the decision to make the promise itself (along with the subsequent action of carrying out the act of promise-making) lacks action-guiding authority. Indeed, imagine trying to shirk a promise by saying, "I was ambivalent when I made it." I don't suspect that excuse will be very convincing to your friend.

What this means is that even if you were ambivalent when you promised your friend that you would help him move, the promise still has action-guiding authority for you, and it still precludes you from failing to deliver on the promise to help. And this is true even if, after making the promise, you look back on your decision with uncertainty or regret, or if you are still not sure that your ordering of motives—the ordering that might have led you make the promise in the first place—is determinate or stable, or if you come to see yourself as being wholly alienated from the motives that moved you to promise in the first place. Ambivalence just isn't the sort of thing that can excuse you from your promissory obligation.

It seems, then, that an ambivalent promise can settle one's will in a way that authoritatively settles the practical question of what to do. Ambivalent promisers might of course still want to insist that they do not fully and decisively or "finally and unequivocally" stand behind the motive that leads them to promise the first place. This is true. But this is also a red herring. What's at stake here is whether ambivalent endorsement of a motive can resolve their will with effective guiding power. And it seems that the ambivalent agent's promise does that even without her *fully* standing behind the choice.

To understand why this is, let's return to your ambivalent promise to help a friend. At a minimum, in order for you to successfully obligate yourself to your friend, your act of promising must have issued from an exercise of your normative competence— your basic ability to appreciate and respond to normatively significant considerations. Duress, coercion, childhood, not being of a "sound mind," etc., all upset agents' normative competence, and they excuse the agent from promissory obligations that they apparently make. But ambivalence does not upset your normative competence—it doesn't render you incapable of appreciating and responding to your friend's obvious need. And when you respond to that obvious need by promising to help, you action must be your own, at least in the following sense: it must be *your* exercise of normative competence that leads to the promise, since "mere heaps of impulses" are not capable of *exercising* a capacity for recognizing and responding to normatively important facts. In short, it is the very act of deciding for a reason that itself suffices to make the action the agent's in the relevant sense.

This does not mean, however, that you are "fully" behind your decision in this case. Nor does it mean that you are unified or wholehearted, as Korsgaard and Frankfurt insist must be the case in order for your movement to be an action. But what it does mean is that an action can be yours even if you do fully stand behind that action. So premise (2) of the Resolution Argument appears to be false.

Unificationists are therefore mistaken to think that a motive is the agent's own only if she has decisively resolved to "finally and un-equivocally" stand behind that motive. Promises that are binding are "the agent's own," even if the agent does not fully stand behind the promise. They are the agent's own because promises are the re-sult of an exercise of normative competence, which is something that only agents and not "mere heaps of impulses" can accomplish. So an action can be your own (in the sense required for autonomy) without you fully standing behind it.

But though I've developed this argument by thinking about promissory obligations, they are not, I think, an isolated case. Rather, this case simply highlights something that is present in other cases: that when an agent's action is the result of an exer-cise of normative competence, it can be her own even if she does not fully stand behind it. Since many of the decisions agents make when faced with ambivalence-inducing practical dilemmas get re-solved through the exercise of normative competence on the part of the agent, those actions will also count as the agents' own, even if the agent does not come to fully stand behind the motive that ulti-mately causes her action.

## 3.6. Resolution without Wholeheartedness

Another key premise, (4), in the unificationists' argument holds that an ambivalent agent fails to decisively resolve the question of which competing motive should cause her movements. Since deci-sive resolution is apparently important for what it is to stand behind one's actions in the way unificationists' imagine to be necessary for autonomy, then this too seems like a real problem for ambiva-lence. But again, unificationists overstate the connection between ambivalence and resolution. You can resolve your will simply by resolving the question "What should I do?" But this sort of resolution is compatible with ambivalence, so again, we'll see that that ambivalence as such poses no threat to self-governance or autonomy.

As it happens, the resources needed to help develop this point were first introduced by Frankfurt himself, who asks us to consider a situation (that he takes to be) analogous to that of an ambivalent individual making a decision: "the situation of someone attempting to solve a problem in arithmetic" (1988, 167). In such a situation, Frankfurt notes that the individual doing the calculation can always worry that he has made a mistake. So what could justify the agent's providing an answer without consulting his calculations *one more time*, just to make sure?

Well, one possibility is that the individual is simply indifferent, and so unmoved by the worry that he might have been negligent or otherwise incompetent in calculating. "I've done it enough, so at this point I don't really care whether I'm right," he might say. But this sort of indifference in the case of our wills, Frankfurt points out, is clearly objectionable. We can't *rationally* resolve a divided will by being indifferent to our own agency in this way.[1]

Another possibility for resolution in the arithmetical case, however, is that the "sequence of calculations might end because the person conducting it *decides for some reason* to adopt a certain result" (Frankfurt 1998, 168). This might either be because "he is unequivocally confident that this result is correct," or "perhaps he believes that even though there is some likelihood that the result is not correct, the cost to him of further inquiry . . . is greater than the value to him of reducing the likelihood of error" (Frankfurt 1998, 168). In either case, Frankfurt thinks that the individual has resolved the problem that arises from his uncertainty about being correct. And this can be extended, Frankfurt tells us, to the

---

[1] For more on this point, see Swindell (2010).

practical realm. Presumably, the idea is simply this: we can resolve our divided will by *deciding for some reason*.

Now Frankfurt himself identifies "decisive commitment" (i.e., deciding for some reason) with being wholehearted, so on first glance, it may not be obvious that this idea supports my contention that we can rationally resolve divisions in our wills without whole-hearted endorsement. But it seems that on this point, Frankfurt is failing to draw the right conclusion from his own lesson. Notice that what resolves the problem in the case of mathematical calcu-lation isn't anything analogous to wholehearted endorsement of an answer.[2] Instead, it's simply that the agent decided *on the basis of reasons* that he was in a position to stop. And of course, in making this decision, the agent does not need to become "finally and un-equivocally clear" about her answer in the arithmetical case, as Frankfurt requires for wholeheartedness, in order to do this.

So while it might also be true of an agent's wholehearted en-dorsement of one of her motives that she does so for a reason, this alone isn't sufficient for wholeheartedness. In order to be whole-hearted, Frankfurt tells us, the agent must also *identify* herself with the motive that she endorses as rationally authoritative. But nothing analogous to "identification" is needed to resolve the question of whether or not one should recalculate. Again, what matters in that case is simply that the individual has decided to stop for a reason, e.g., because he thinks he's been suitably careful in his calculations to merit giving up on endlessly repeating them for the sake of per-fect (and unattainable) certainty. It seems, then, that if we're to take Frankfurt's analogy seriously, we can jettison his insistence on wholeheartedness because something much less demanding can do the trick. An ambivalent agent can resolve the practical question of what to do (i.e., of which motive to act on) as long as the de-cision she makes is made for reasons, even if the agent does not

---

[2] Indeed, what would wholehearted endorsement even look like in this context?

wholeheartedly identify her practical self with the motives that are responding to those reasons.[3]

This means that, for example, when I feel ambivalent about grading students' papers—I have other important demands on my time, after all, and careful attention to students' work is very time consuming—resolving the practical question of what to do is possible without any wholehearted endorsement on my part, so long as I choose as I do *for reasons*. This is because, as Frankfurt pointed out in the case of mathematical calculation, reasons confer action-guiding authority to my decisions: once I've reasonably chosen to grade student papers, I now have reasons to continue to do so even after my motivation to continue flags. That is, the initial reason upon which I decide and my subsequent decision to act on the basis of that reason are together generative of new reasons for action. But in deciding to grade papers rather than working on another project, I need not have excised my ambivalence—I certainly don't need to be finally or unequivocally behind my choice. Indeed, I need not have become wholehearted in any way, since I can still recognize that my desire to get other work done is as much a part of me as the desire to take my students' papers seriously.

Now you might think that this case is a problem for Frankfurt only because I am treating this case as a conflict of identifying rather than a conflict of willing. According to this objection, although my decision for reasons doesn't require that I resolve my ambivalence in the way that is required by conflicts of identifying

---

[3] Of course, not just *any* reason will suffice; you must settle your will for the *right* kinds of reasons. But this is no different than in the arithmetical case. For in that case, you won't want to decide to stop for just any ol' reason—that you're tired or bored, for example, or that you're indifferent about being correct. Only reasons of the sort Frankfurt invokes (e.g., that given your competence in basic arithmetic, the likelihood of error is low enough to move on) will legitimate the decision to stop. Analogously, in the practical case, one will want to select a course of action on the basis of the reasons that make that course of action choiceworthy (in cases of conflict between merely permissible courses of action) or rationally necessary (in cases in which one possible course of action is rationally required). Thus, the mere fact that one option is, for example, more convenient or less taxing will not typically be a reason that will resolve the agent's will.

(viz., the extrusion or outlawing of one of the motives), it *does* require me to prioritize one motive over the other in a stable and determinate ordering. In other words, you might think that I have failed to recognize that in this case, the conflict at stake is actually a conflict of willing and *not* a conflict of identifying. As a result, resolution in this case will only require that I am able to integrate my preferences into a single list that determinately specifies which preferences have priority.

This is perhaps right, though I think that reflecting on what it would mean for competing motives to be "integrated into a single ordering, within which each occupies a specific position" (Frankfurt 1988, 170), might be instructive at this point. After all, it's not entirely clear what this sort of integration requires. In the case at hand, does it only mean that I am able to order the two competing motives, irrespective of other motives that I might have? Could I, for example, achieve integration by ranking the motive that leads me to grade papers (call this my "grading" motive) as having more authority than the motive that leads me to work on other projects (my "other projects" motive)? Perhaps. But notice: this ordering will only make sense given a contingent background of other motives that we're holding fixed, as well as more general background conditions. For instance, it's only near the end of the term that this conflict even arises. In October and February, respectively, it doesn't make sense for me to be overly concerned with getting things graded. This suggests that the ordering is conditional or defeasible in a way that will allow for me to not always sublimate my "other projects" motive to my "grading" motive—e.g., possibly, the list needs a temporal indexing of some sort.

However, even granting the defeasible priority of my "grading" motive at the end of terms, it's not—nor should it be—*determinate* that the "grading" motive has necessary priority over the "other projects" motive. If I owe a paper to an editor, or have revisions that are due, then maybe I'll work on those projects rather than grading, even if it's the end of term. And certainly, if something comes up with one of my daughters, I'll put off grading for a time. But these exceptions (which are easily multipliable) suggest that special circumstances can also trump the defeasible priority of "grading" motives. At this point, though, it's not clear that I've really "integrated" anything onto a single list. Rather, I seem to recognize that given these two motives, along with all of the other motives and values that are part of who I am as an agent, I have reasons to do things that sometimes conflict. And the weightiness of these reasons depends not only on the intrinsic choiceworthiness of the ends themselves, but also on the context in which the conflict occurs: *is it at the beginning of a term or near the end; is everything okay with my family; am I coming up for tenure; am I coming up for tenure but already secure when it comes to "excellence in research"; have I promised someone a draft of a paper by a certain date; is there a global pandemic; etc.*

The kind of deliberative flexibility that is required here suggests that an appropriate way to deal with the conflict is not to definitively or invariably order one's motives, but is to instead adopt a more particularist approach.[4] Very plausibly, I can recognize that in *this* context one motive has priority while also acknowledging that in another context—perhaps even a fairly similar context—the other motive would have priority.

It is possible that this is consistent with Frankfurt's account of what needs to be done in order to resolve ambivalence in conflicts of willing. But notice that if it is, then Frankfurt's technical notions of "wholeheartedness" and "decisive commitment" no longer reflect our ordinary conceptions of these concepts.[5] After all, on this reading, to be wholehearted in the face of conflicts of willing, an agent need not be unified or finally and unequivocally committed.

---

[4] In particular, what seems important for settling these questions is not some prearranged list, but an exercise of normative competence. For more on this point, see Jonathan Dancy (2004).

[5] Timothy Schroeder and Nomy Arpaly (1999) raise a similar worry about Frankfurt's notions of alienation and externality.

She doesn't even have to be definitive in ordering the competing motives. Nor do those motives really need to be "integrated" at all. All she needs is to decide for a reason (of the right sort). Crucially, this suggests that the agent need not excise her ambivalence in order to resolve conflicts of this sort. On this interpretation of Frankfurt's notion of resolution, then, the phenomenon I've identified with ambivalence in Chapter 2 would be consistent with a certain kind of wholeheartedness, and, consequently, it would be no threat (even by Frankfurt's lights) to our autonomous agency. It seems, then, that Frankfurt's ideal of wholeheartedness either is not in conflict with ambivalence, or is in conflict with ambivalence only because Frankfurt insists upon a flawed account of what's required to resolve one's will in the face of practical conflicts. But in neither of these cases, I submit, do we have reason to think ambivalence is a threat to autonomy.

A related problem for Frankfurt's view emerges even more clearly in conflicts of identifying—e.g., the case that Frankfurt considers in which a man is radically ambivalent about his love for a woman. To fill in that case, let's suppose the man is ambivalent about his feelings for an old friend he has come to recognize as being extremely untrustworthy. He genuinely loves her and he also thinks that he shouldn't love her; indeed, we can imagine that when he thinks of the things she has done to betray his trust, he is repulsed by the thought of continuing to love her and be her friend. So on the one hand, his love for his friend renders him alienated from the motives and tendencies that led him to conclude that he shouldn't love her, while on the other hand, these latter motives and tendencies simultaneously render him alienated from his love for her. Accordingly, he is ambivalent about the question of how he should feel about her, as well as the question of what he should do about his relationship with her.

But suppose that he weighs the reasons for and against continuing the friendship, and he decides that he has sufficient grounds for ending it, even though it meant a great deal to him over many long years. And suppose that on the basis of this deliberation, he ends the friendship. On its face, it seems that the decision the man arrives at in deliberation and subsequently executes resolves his will in an action-guiding way. Yet nothing about this process necessarily involves the man extruding as outlaw the love he still has toward his old friend. That is, nothing about the process of decisively resolving to end the friendship requires that he see his continued valuing of the friend as somehow foreign to his agency. Nor is it the case that by resolving the practical conflict he faces, the agent "finally and unequivocally" stands behind the decision to end the friendship. He is, it seems, both divided and resolved.

Naturally, this sort of resolution won't eliminate the man's psychic distress or stave off the regret that he might feel in those circumstances. Nor can it guarantee that the man won't feel alienated to some degree from his decision, which is a consequence of the fact that the man still identifies himself with his love for a longtime friend.[6] But these facts are ultimately immaterial, since even wholehearted endorsement of one option over the other couldn't do *that*. Recall, Frankfurt himself happily concedes that even after an agent has wholeheartedly resolved himself, "the forces mobilized on the other may persist with as much intensity as before" (2004, 91). Rather, all that's needed to show that the Resolution Argument is unsound is something more minimal: that the ambivalent agent can resolve the practical conflict in his will in an authoritatively action-guiding way. And plausibly the man's decision to end the friendship on the basis of reasons is action-guiding in just this way, even if he ultimately remains ambivalent about that decision.

[6] It's worth noting, however, that it's not altogether clear that being psychologically alienated from one's motives is necessarily bad. As Peter Railton (1984) has pointed out, morality sometimes requires this of us. And no doubt it's not just morality, but also our love for others and for our own selves, that will almost surely make it rationally required of us that we sometimes feel alienated (and so "unresolved" in that sense) from the motives that we act on.

Here the unificationist might object. Sure, it's *possible* that an ambivalent agent can resolve her will. But isn't it clearly better that the will be resolved wholeheartedly? In the case Frankfurt considers, for example, although it might be true that the man can resolve his will by deciding for reasons, doesn't it seem preferable that he does so in a way that excises his ambivalence fully? Perhaps he recognizes that embracing whatever choice he makes would be for the best—that either choice would go better if it doesn't leave him tied up in knots over "the road not taken." Of course, this wouldn't show that ambivalence *must* be excised to resolve conflicts within the will. But it does show something that is friendly to the spirit of unificationists: that it's *optimal* or *ideal* for agents to excise ambivalence from their will.

There are two things to say in response to this final objection. First, it's important to note that nothing I've said should be construed as an argument that wholeheartedness as such is bad. On the contrary, I do think it's often a good thing that agents are wholehearted in their decisions. For example, it can be good to be wholehearted in cases in which focus or single-mindedness or unequivocal commitment is necessary for success. It can also be good to be wholehearted in cases in which continued ambivalence would literally undermine an individual's psychological health or well-being. In each of these cases, though, it is *instrumentally* good that the agent is wholehearted. That is, in these cases at least, the fact that she is wholehearted in these cases isn't directly germane to whether the agent is autonomous.

But this is precisely what is going on in the case considered above. If Frankfurt's man both wants to love and does not want to love his friend, he must decide whether to continue the friendship. And if either alternative would be sufficiently good, then it seems he has good reasons for going either way. But once he makes the decision, say, to end the friendship, then he has reason to put it behind him for the sake managing his life going forward. This, of course, isn't to say that he has no reason to be ambivalent; it's instead to recognize that the value of getting on with his life is sufficiently great as to make it reasonable for him to take steps to not be ambivalent. To do otherwise, we can imagine, would make him worse off in a variety of ways. But it would not, I think, make him a failure qua agent, since what matters for that is that he exercises his normative competence and makes a decision on the basis of reasons, and this is consistent with continued ambivalence on his part.

The second thing to say here is that the sort of resolution that ambivalent agents are able to come to is sometimes clearly better than wholehearted alternatives—not just instrumentally better, but genuinely more responsive to the values at stake (and so, more reflective of normative competence). We see this perhaps most clearly in cases of what Hili Razinsky has called "compromise actions." Razinsky illustrates such cases as follows:

> Let us consider a person who wishes and does not wish to practice law. He wants to be a lawyer only in order to satisfy his parents' expectations. For his own part, he would rather devote his life to literature. He finds a firm that is willing, in exchange for a low salary and non-advancement, to hire him a part-time capacity, and in working there he realizes a compromise between his two desires. (Razinsky 2017, 250)

In this case, we have an agent who, because of his love for his parents, wants to be a lawyer and, because of his own goals and ambitions, does not want to do that. And in order to resolve his will, he compromises each of these concerns. So what we see here is not wholehearted resolution but a form of resolution that enables the agent to live with the incompatible desires. Notice, however, that in Razinsky's case, it seems plausible that the part-time lawyer has done a better job of respecting his inner concerns than he would have had he committed wholeheartedly to practicing law or to abandoning it. And again, the sense in which he's done "better" isn't that by compromising, he's just done a better job of bringing about a good or pleasurable state of affairs; it's rather that he's done a better job of acting in a way that adequately respects who he is as an agent.

What this means is that it's not enough for the unificationist to concede that ambivalent agents can resolve their wills while also insisting that wholehearted resolution is nevertheless better. Instead, they owe us an argument that this is so, and that argument must respect both the fact that instrumental value is not what's at stake in these debates and the fact that in cases of compromise actions (at the very least), the kind of resolution possible for ambivalent agents more closely adheres to the standards of well-functioning agency.

## 3.7. Conclusion

The claim that underlies the Resolution Argument is that in the absence of resolution, ambivalence precludes the sort of "final and unequivocal" endorsement of the motive that causes an agent's movements and that, as a result, it precludes autonomy and self-governed action. In other words, the worry that leads one to unificationism here is that if we are ambivalent, then we are not *free* in an important sense. And just as freedom from internal strife is necessary for a political body to flourish, so too, you might think that freedom from ambivalence is necessary for agents to flourish.

But though these claims have an initial plausibility, they overstate the connections between autonomy and self-governance on the one hand with resolution, unity, and wholeheartedness on the other. Instead, what matters for autonomy—what makes our actions *ours*—is that they are the result of an exercise of the normative competence that makes us the rational agents we are. But ambivalence does not threaten this. Indeed, as I'll argue in the second half the book, our ambivalence is often required by normative competence, and so in that way ambivalence rather than wholeheartedness can signify well-functioning agency.

# 4

# Affirmation and Ambivalence

## 4.1. The Heaviest Weight?

Late in *Gay Science*, Friedrich Nietzsche invites us to consider a scenario that is either terrifying or electrifying (or both!).

> What if some day or night a demon were to steal into your loneliest loneliness and say to you: "This life as you now live it and have lived it you will have to live once again and innumerable times again; and there will be nothing new in it, but every pain and every job and every thought and sigh and everything unspeakably small or great in your life must return to you, all in the same succession and sequence—even this spider and this moonlight between the trees, and even this moment and I myself. The eternal hourglass of existence is turned over again and again, and you with it, speck of dust!" Would you not throw yourself down and gnash your teeth and curse the demon who spoke thus? Or have you once experienced a tremendous moment when you would have answered him: "You are a god, and never have I heard anything more divine." If this thought gained power over you, as you are it would transform and possibly crush you; the question in each and every thing, "Do you want this again and innumerable times again?" would lie on your actions as the heaviest weight! Or how well disposed would you have to become to yourself and to life *to long for nothing more fervently* than for this ultimate eternal confirmation and seal? (2001, §341)

*In Praise of Ambivalence*. D. Justin Coates, Oxford University Press. © Oxford University Press 2023.
DOI: 10.1093/oso/9780197652398.003.0004

Here, along with passages in *Thus Spoke Zarathustra*,[1] Nietzsche presents his so-called doctrine of eternal recurrence. How exactly to interpret this passage and its companion passages is a matter of some controversy among Nietzsche scholars. But two general ways of thinking about eternal recurrence have emerged. On the first of these, Nietzsche is understood as proposing a cosmological thesis about how the world actually is. On the second view, around which some consensus has developed (see Magnus 1978; Nehamas 1980; Clarke 1990, etc.), these passages present us with an existentialist or practical challenge by inviting us to reorient how we determine and evaluate the choices that we make.

Though I won't pretend to settle this thorny debate here, I will note that the scholarly consensus that has emerged in the past forty years seems well founded. It is based, at least in part, on the simple fact that one need not accept the cosmological interpretation of the eternal recurrence in order to appreciate the rhetorical and argumentative significance the doctrine plays in Nietzsche's later work (see, e.g., Soll 1973). And if you can reasonably interpret the doctrine as a heuristic—a thought experiment designed to make us reflect on what we value—without needing to understand Nietzsche as thereby committing himself to a bizarre cosmological thesis, why wouldn't you? Thus for our current purposes, which are primarily philosophical rather than purely exegetical in scope, the doctrine of the eternal recurrence will be understood simply as proposing a significant existentialist or practical challenge.[2]

---

[1] See especially *Zarathustra* III, 2, 13 (Nietzsche 1995).

[2] To be clear, properly adjudicating this controversy is beyond my ken. Nevertheless, I do think that it would be *disappointing* if Nietzsche were exclusively (or even primarily) making a cosmological point here. Such a view seems dubious on its face as a hypothesis about space and time. Moreover, the alternative interpretation of these passages makes for an incredibly rich and possibly profound picture of what a good life looks like for human persons. Disappointment is, of course, a bad principle on which to base historical scholarship. So what follows shouldn't be understood as a definite "take" on Nietzsche's doctrine of eternal recurrence. Instead, I'm exploring a genuinely interesting philosophical possibility that is at least suggested by Nietzsche's text and welcomed by a wide array of commentators.

## 4.2. Affirmation and the Dionysian Attitude

But what sort of challenge or test is it? And what does it reveal
about the individuals who accept the challenge or take the test?
In response to these questions, Aaron Ridley sums up what
I take to be the core commitment of the existentialist/practical
interpretation:

> It is clear that the thought of eternal recurrence is being prosed
> as a test of some kind, a thought experiment which will somehow
> sort the sheep from the goats. And one passes the test, it seems, if
> one can experience the thought as maximally welcome; one fails
> if one falls to the floor and starts gnashing one's teeth. (1997, 19)

On this view, which Ridley clearly states, Nietzsche poses this scenario because he thinks that the attitude we would take to the possibility of eternal recurrence illuminates something important about
the worthiness of our choices, characters, and lives as a whole. But
what is this thing? What makes us, as Ridley puts it, sheep rather
than goats?

Maudemarie Clark provides some insight here.

> Nietzsche [is] taking our hypothetical reaction to the demon's
> message—how we would reactive if we accepted the message
> uncritically—to reflect our actual attitude towards ourselves and
> our lives. A joyful reaction would indicate a fully affirmative at-
> titude towards one's (presumably, nonrecurring) life, whereas
> gnashing of teeth, and the need to ask "do you want this once
> more and innumerable times more?" would indicate a negative
> attitude. There can be no doubt that Nietzsche wants to promote
> the former attitude. . . . [T]he recurrence cosmology provides
> a device for articulating Nietzsche's ideal of the life-affirming
> person. This ideal person satisfies what Nietzsche calls "the idea
> of eternal recurrence," the "highest formula of affirmation that is

at all attainable." The formula of affirmation provided by eternal recurrence is that of being a person who would respond joyfully to the demon's message if she accepted it uncritically as the truth. . . . Nietzsche's doctrine of eternal recurrence [is] the presentation of such affirmation as an ideal for human beings. (1990, 251–52)

Brian Leiter concurs with Clark's interpretation, and in so doing, tells us a bit more about *what* exactly is being tested for: whether one is a "higher type,"—i.e., whether one "evinces what Nietzsche often calls a 'Dionysian' or 'life-affirming' attitude" (Leiter 2015, 96). What this means, Leiter suggests, is that

a person, for Nietzsche, has a *Dionysian attitude* toward life insofar as he affirms his life unconditionally; in particular, insofar as he affirms it *including* the "suffering" or other hardships it has involved. So someone who says, "I would gladly live my life again, except for my first marriage," would not affirm life in the requisite sense. Thus, we may say that a person *affirms* his life in Nietzsche's sense only insofar as he would gladly will its eternal return: i.e., will the repetition of his entire life through eternity. Nietzsche calls "the idea of the eternal recurrence" the "highest formulation of affirmation that is at all attainable." Higher men, then, are marked by a distinctive Dionysian attitude toward their life: they would gladly will the repetition of their life eternally. (2015, 96)

In other words, Nietzsche is, in essence, recommending to us a specific conception of an *ideal* life or an *ideal* form of agency. On this view, our lives are good and our decisions well made just in case we can affirm them *as they are* and in their totality.

At this point, it seems clear that the Dionysian attitude is deeply opposed to ambivalence. After all, it seems that in order to take this attitude toward your life it's not enough that you affirm your life on balance as being worthy of repeated livings. You must instead fully embrace your life as a whole, including the "bad" elements, since they are no less integral to your life than are the "good" elements. This is why, Leiter claims, it's not enough to want to live your life again *sans* a bad first marriage. Real affirmation—affirmation of the sort that higher types practice—thus demands that a person take an unequivocal attitude toward her life as a whole. In other words, real affirmation demands that we be *wholehearted* in our endorsement of our lives.

Nietzsche's *Dionysian attitude* also seems to require that we not be ambivalent during our lives. We could imagine, for example, that after taking the new job, Erica looks at her life happily, thinking that she made a good choice to take the job opportunity, even though it meant living far away from her family. But she might also think that it would have been a good choice to stay close to her loved ones. And she might think her life would have been no worse—and certainly no less affirmable—had she chosen differently. Here her affirmation seems less definitive and more halfhearted, owing to the fact that she is not uniquely affirming her life as it has gone thus far.

Moreover, Erica might, in a moment of uncritical acceptance of the truth of the demon's message, reasonably prefer to live her life otherwise given another chance to do so. This halfheartedness on Erica's part will, of course, be multiplied by the fact that for most of us, there is not only one moment of ambivalence that we confront in our lives that singularly defines them. More commonly, we are faced with many such moments, and so even if we are in some meaningful sense happy with our actual lives, we are also sufficiently alive to unrealized alternatives as to make those possibilities enticing as well. So at best, any affirmation that the ambivalent agent can muster will be tempered by the fact that her will is indeterminate and that she does not "finally and unequivocally" stand behind her choices, even if she recognizes that they did work out. Yet this doesn't seem to be enough, at least not for Nietzsche. Nor will it suffice, as we'll see below, for Frankfurt.

## 4.3. Nietzsche's Unificationism

But before turning to Frankfurt's alternative account of the connection between affirmation and well-functioning agency, I want to head off a legitimate worry you might have about this line of thinking when applied to Nietzsche's account of affirmation. Nietzsche is famously sensitive to the fact that human motivation is not always (or ever) guided by Reason, and so he is not inclined to see *unification* in the sense Plato and Augustine and Kant and Korsgaard value, where our unruly motives are brought into some kind of consistency and subservience to our rational appreciation of the good, or to God's will, or to the law of rational agency. Instead, he seems happy to admit that we have many distinctive "drives and affects" (Nietzsche 2003, §19) that structure our behavior, and not always in a coherent or logical way.

Moreover, as Brian Leiter (2007) has argued, there is perhaps reason to doubt that Nietzsche accepts a form of human agency about which it makes sense to say that *the agent can finally and unequivocally stand behind what she does*. Indeed, this phrasing is suggestive of an irreducible seat of agential powers that lurks behind our motivational and evaluative orientations. But this is dubious, Leiter argues, given the accounts of agency and freedom Nietzsche (2003) develops in *Beyond Good and Evil* §§19 and 21. On Leiter's interpretation, then, it seems that there are no agents—at least not in any meaningful sense—about whom the ideal of unification *or* the malady of ambivalence can sensibly apply.

A complete and systematic response to this objection is simply outside the scope of this current project, but I do want to say a few things to suggest that Nietzsche can plausibly be read as a unificationist, albeit perhaps a unique one in many ways. The first thing to note is that although Nietzsche is deeply skeptical of "'freedom of the will' in the superlative metaphysical sense" (2003, §21), it's much less clear that Nietzsche is skeptical of agency as such, or even of positive and negative appraisals we can make on how people exercise their wills. Although such appraisals are not to be identified with praise or blame in the traditional sense, Nietzsche tells us later on in the same passage that they do mark the *strength* or *weakness* of an agent's will.[3] And this suggests that he does in fact have some conception of human persons as agents, since our wills can only be contrasted as strong or weak against some background standard or expectation that we have of ourselves. But having a background standard or expectation of how people will or should exercise their wills only makes sense if we are—at least in some attenuated sense—agents. Moreover, it is difficult to see how Nietzsche could recommend the Dionysian attitude and life-affirmation as the highest ideal for human persons if we are not agents in any meaningful sense. After all, why should a person's affirmation of her life matter, if the affirmation cannot be properly attributed to her?

It is for this reason that I think Leiter's *eliminativist* interpretation of Nietzsche's action theory goes too far. It is better, I submit, to interpret Nietzsche's account of willing in *Beyond Good and Evil* §19 as *reductivist* instead. This interpretation preserves Leiter's insight that Nietzsche's naturalism is at odds with the idea that there is a magical, irreducible faculty, *the will*, which lurks behind all of our choices. But it also squares with what Nietzsche does earlier in *Beyond Good and Evil*. In *Beyond Good and Evil* §12, for example, he offers a reductive account of the soul, and suggests that, in general, this sort of reduction is the project that "new psychologists" should engage in.

In that passage he first rejects traditional analyses of the soul— "We must put an end to that other and more disastrous atomism, the one Christianity has taught best and longest, the *atomism of the soul*. . . . *this* belief must be thrown out of science!" (2003, §12). He then immediately shifts gears, intimating, as if to a co-conspirator:

---

[3] For more on this distinction as it arises in Nietzsche's philosophy of action, see Gemes 2009 and Kirwin 2017. For more on (roughly) the distinction itself, see Watson 1996.

Between you and me, there is absolutely no need to give up "the soul" itself, and relinquish one of the oldest and most venerable hypotheses—as often happens with naturalists: given their clumsiness, they barely need to touch "the soul" to lose it. But the path lies open for new version and sophistications of the soul hypothesis—and concepts like the "mortal soul" and the "soul as subject-multiplicity" and the "soul as a society constructed out of drives and affects" want henceforth to have civil rights in the realm of science. By putting an end to the superstition that until now has grown around the idea of the soul with an almost tropical luxuriance, the *new* psychologist clearly thrust himself into a new wasteland and a new suspicion. (2003, §12)

So for Nietzsche, it is a mistake to think that the soul is an indivisible atom or monad. But the naturalist commitments that lead Nietzsche to reach this conclusion aren't so clumsy as to make us think that this means there is no such thing as a soul. Instead, Nietzsche suggests that what the soul is can be reduced to more basic psychological elements. It is, he contends, a society or political order that is composed out of our motivational drives and feelings.

It seems plausible to me, then, that something analogous is going on in *Beyond Good and Evil* §§19 and 21. The ideas of the "will" and "acts of willing" have undoubtedly been used and abused by traditional doctrines. But rather than throwing out those ideas altogether, Nietzsche can be understood as offering us a reductive account in terms of the functional roles that our underlying drives and affects play in structuring our behavior. In other words, this interpretation of Nietzsche on the will leaves room for the will in a properly naturalist moral psychology.

Of course, more needs to be said to fully unpack the details of Nietzsche's theory. On this point, recent scholarship is helpful. For example, Maudemarie Clark and David Dudrick (2012) argue that Nietzsche regards the inner *political* or *normative* ordering of an agent's drives, particularly their relative ranks as commanding and obedient drives respectively, as being the basis of an agent's values. And accordingly, this ordering is also the basis for action's being *hers*, since action will be an agent's own when the agent exercises her normative competence and, as a result, is moved to act in a way that responds to what her values require of her. The kind of internal harmony between commanding and obedient drives that Clark and Dudrick identify is therefore crucial for strength of will, which for Nietzsche seems to be among the highest appraisals one can make about an agent.

By contrast, Paul Katsafanas interprets Nietzsche as offering a non-normative alternative account of valuing according to which "an agent values X iff the agent (1) has a drive-induced positive affective orientation toward X, and (2) does not disapprove of this affective orientation" (Katsafanas 2016, 120). Here it seems what would be required for an action to be caused by her values (and therefore one she stands behind) is that there not be internal strife between her affective orientation and her attitude toward that orientation. So the relevant kind of unity achieved on this view is not the unity achieved when a platoon obeys its sergeant's commands, as Clark and Dudrick claim. Instead, it is a unity between one's general "orientation" toward something (and courses of action that promote, honor, or respect that thing) and the agent's higher-order attitudes, attitudes like approval.

The differences between the kind of unificationism that emerges from Clark and Dudrick's and Katsafanas's respective interpretations notwithstanding, I think each of these makes it clear that there are resources in Nietzsche for interpreting him in a way that allows humans to have a robust form of agency—one that involves genuine evaluative engagement on the part of human agents with their worlds. And indeed, you might think it is precisely because we are evaluative creatures—however this power is manifested in our will—that affirmation, an intrinsically agential activity, seems meaningful in the way that Nietzsche suggests.

However, even if it turns out that Leiter's eliminativist Nietzsche *just was* the actual Nietzsche, this doesn't ultimately undermine the idea—call it "Nietzschean" if you prefer—that unequivocal life-affirmation is a key constituent of an ideal kind of life for human agents. And this idea is, I submit, an attractive ideal in its own right, independently of whether it is Nietzsche's idea or *merely* Nietzschean. Because of this, and because something akin to the Dionysian ideal of life-affirmation has been developed and defended in other venues, it's one that anti-unificationists such as myself must reckon with.

## 4.4.  Wholeheartedness and Self-Satisfaction

The *Dionysian attitude* that Nietzsche champions as being the sign of an ideal form of life bears striking similarity to Harry Frankfurt's conception of self-love.[4] According to Frankfurt:

> Insofar as a person love himself—in other words, to the extent that he is volitionally wholehearted—he does not resist any movement of his own will. He is not at odds with himself; he does not oppose, or seek to impede, the expression in practical reasoning and in conduct of whatever love his self-love entails. He is free in loving what he loves, at least in the sense that his loving is not obstructed or interfered with by himself.
>
> Self-love has going for it, then, its role in constituting both the structure of volitional rationality and the mode of freedom that this structure of the will ensures. Loving ourselves is desirable and important for us because it is the same thing, more or less, as being *satisfied with ourselves*. The self-satisfaction to which it

---

[4] As it happens, Frankfurt's long-term project has been to develop reductive accounts of the self, the will, and freedom of the will. He thus seems to be a "new psychologist" in Nietzsche's sense.

> is equivalent is . . . a condition in which we *willingly accept and endorse our own volitional identity*. We are content with the final goals and with the loving by which our will is most penetratingly defined. (2004, 97; emphasis added)

We see here a striking similarity between the Dionysian attitude of affirmation and Frankfurt's notion of self-satisfaction in particular. The individual who *affirms* her life is one who wholeheartedly endorses every element of it—every choice and every outcome that that choice leads to. The individual who is *self-satisfied* is someone who loves herself, in the sense that she is "volitionally wholehearted"; i.e., she is finally and unequivocally committed to the motives that comprise her practical identity. What's more, her willingness to accept and endorse her innermost motives itself seems to be a form of affirmation, affirming not her life as a whole necessarily, as Nietzsche's higher types affirm, but simply who she is as an agent. And just as Nietzsche is plausibly interpreted as claiming that the Dionysian attitude is an ideal for human beings, Frankfurt similarly claims that self-love and satisfaction "may well be the 'highest' or most important thing[s] of all" (2004, 98 n. 80).

Of course, it's important to note that there are also some differences between these ideals of a human life and of human agency respectively. Whereas Nietzsche propounds the Dionysian attitude of affirmation without caveat, Frankfurt is happy to concede that self-love and the satisfaction with oneself that it can foster are not sufficient for an ideal or even good *life* as a whole. Citing Spinoza, who regards self-love and self-satisfaction as being "really the highest thing we can hope for" (*Ethics* 4.52S), Frankfurt admits that this will not suffice to render our lives good or guarantee our welfare.

> After all, being satisfied with oneself is consistent with being disappointed at how things turn out, with a recognition that we have failed in what we tried most earnestly to do, and with the

unhappiness that such misfortunes naturally bring. . . . The fact
that we are satisfied with ourselves does not entail being satisfied with our lives. Nevertheless, perhaps Spinoza is right. Loving
oneself may well be the "highest" or the most important thing of
all. (2004, 97–98 n. 8)

Thus while Frankfurt does indeed regard self-satisfaction as absolutely crucial for ideal agency, he stops short of thinking that this
type of affirmation will guarantee a good life more generally.

Additionally, Frankfurt is quite a bit clearer that he means for
his ideal to be incompatible with ambivalence. So while I think it's
highly doubtful that you could adopt the Dionysian attitude toward
your life as a whole if your life was marked by instances of deep
and trenchant ambivalence, it is positively impossible to be satisfied with yourself in the way Frankfurt describes if you are volitionally fragmented. If you experience necessary inner faction, if you
find yourself unable to resolve your will without significant value
remainder, then on Frankfurt's view, you are failing to love yourself. The reason for this, Frankfurt thinks, is that loving someone
involves caring for her welfare in a disinterested way. And if you
cared for your own welfare in a disinterested way, you would want
to be free of internal strife. As a result, you would want to have a
coherent, unified inner life that is peaceful, harmonious, and unified. You would want your will to be, in other words, "volitionally
wholehearted." Self-love and, thus, the kind of endorsement only a
satisfied person can make of her will are necessarily out of reach for
the ambivalent agent.

## 4.5. Two Affirmation Arguments

Of course, for our purposes, these differences in the scope and
strength of Nietzsche's and Frankfurt's respective claims about affirmation and satisfaction are of little consequence. If one (or both)

of these theories articulates a meaningful ideal of human life or agency—one that we have reason to care about and strive for—then we must excise ambivalence from our wills to the degree that is possible. The Nietzschean argument for this conclusion turns on the crucial idea that only wholehearted or definite or unequivocal affirmation of your life as a whole suffices for the kind of affirmation that secures the highest good for it. Frankfurt's argument for this conclusion also requires that you be satisfied with yourself, which in turn requires that you "willingly accept and endorse" the motives that comprise the innermost elements of your practical identity. But neither wholehearted affirmation of your life nor willing acceptance and endorsement of your practical identity is on the table for ambivalent agents. To live a life that is meaningful and one in which you can be truly satisfied with oneself, your practical identity cannot be fragmented but must instead be unified.

These points have significant importance for our accounts of well-functioning agency even though they are targeting first and foremost the incompatibility of ambivalence with *meaning* and *satisfaction* respectively. Living meaningfully or living in a way that you can be satisfied with yourself is of course a property different from the property of being a well-functioning agent. Yet it would be surprising if their instantiation conditions were not highly correlated. And it would be downright bizarre if their instantiation conditions were incompatible, such that to live a meaningful life, you must be a failure qua agent, or that to be a well-functioning agent, you must give up on living meaningfully or in a self-satisfying way. By this reasoning, if Nietzsche and Frankfurt are right in thinking that meaning and self-satisfaction each require a form of affirmation that is incompatible with ambivalence, it would be highly unlikely that openness to ambivalence is somehow key to well-functioning agency. It would be much more plausible, assuming the importance of wholehearted affirmation for meaning and self-satisfaction, that unification would mark well-functioning or ideal forms human agency.

So: Nietzsche's and Frankfurt's arguments are important. But are they sound? To begin answering this question, I first want to consider why one might care about affirmation in the first place. What could it have to do with a meaningful, higher-type life or with loving oneself? There are two chief possibilities here. First, it might be that affirmation *makes* it the case that one's life comes to be meaningful. On this view, it is because you respond to the demon's message with wholehearted affirmation that your actual life has meaning. Affirmation would be, in other words, a meaning *generator*. A second way in which affirmation might be important is that because one will be disposed to unequivocally affirm one's life *if* it does in fact have meaning, a thought experiment of the sort Nietzsche develops in *Gay Science* §341 provides us with a clear way of answering the question of whether our lives are meaningful. On this alternative, affirmation as such does not necessarily bring about or generate meaning, but it does reveal it where it is already present.

As I understand Nietzsche, it seems plausible that he would clearly reject the second of these alternatives, owing to the fact that he denies the existence of intrinsic, objective value. As a consequence, there is not some value that affirmation can merely track or alert us to. So, for Nietzsche, if there is indeed a connection between affirmation and a meaningful life of the sort higher types enjoy, it must be because affirmation itself confers value on one's life and one's choices.

For Frankfurt, the interpretative question is less clear-cut. Frankfurt is a Humean about practical reasons, in that he thinks that our caring about something itself generates reasons for action, independently of the intrinsic properties of the thing in question. So because he accepts that the innermost elements of our psychologies—what we care about—can generate reasons for action, it would not be too much of a leap to understand Frankfurt as claiming that wholehearted affirmation, which is a form of affirmation that unequivocally expresses the unity of our inner selves, similarly generates the " 'highest' or most important thing" (Frankfurt 2004, 98 n. 8) for agents.

Yet, despite this parallel to his account of practical reasons, I think that for Frankfurt, this gets things backward. An agent's wholehearted endorsement of her "volitional identity" manifests or reveals the underlying state of her soul—that she unequivocally loves herself—and it is for this reason that she is satisfied and contented with who she is as agent. So here, affirmation does not confer value or meaning for the agent so much as reflect the fact that the agent already enjoys the kind of self-love that the value in question consists in. In other words, the agent who loves herself will fervently approve of the demon's message, but this approval is not *why* she can be said to enjoy "the highest thing we can hope for," but a manifestation of the fact that she already enjoys that thing, and so takes pleasure at the thought of its eternal recurrence.

Here we have two possibilities for understanding why fervent or wholehearted affirmation is necessary for a property that one might reasonably think to be deeply tied to meaningfulness. On the first of these, which is Nietzschean in its orientation, affirmation is necessary for meaningfulness because it confers it. On the second of these, which comes from Harry Frankfurt, self-love and contentment with yourself—two properties we might well think to be closely connected to meaningfulness—entail a willingness on your part to unequivocally affirm your *self*. But while both of these claims have some initial plausibility, ultimately, neither is true. So on neither interpretation is the Affirmation Argument's key premise true.

### 4.5.1. Why Affirmation Matters: A Nietzschean Account

As I see it, there is something very appealing about the Nietzschean account of why affirmation matters. Some of its appeal is certainly due to the fact that there seems to be something normatively significant about affirmation. In particular, it just seems that in many ordinary cases, affirmation confers value on the object of affirmation. And the type of value it seems to confer is one that is especially central to discussions of a good or meaningful life: value *for the agent*. We think, after all, that a good or meaningful life must be good or meaningful for the agent herself. So affirmation apparently matters for a good or meaningful life.

But it is not obvious why this is so. Why does the fact that I affirm my life or affirm some activity make it the case that my life or that activity now has value for me? One possibility is that affirmation confers an additional form of value. So, for example, it seems that even if I believe there to be some value, be it wholly impersonal or particular only to some subset of people, to watching soccer games, that judgment does not necessarily commit me to caring about soccer or as regarding it as valuable to me. There are, after all, many things that I think of as having some value that I don't really care about or value. In addition to soccer, we can add opera, poetry, double IPAs, and cinema in either its high- or low-brow forms to the list. Of course, if I decide to broaden my horizon and develop a new hobby or interest, I can make it the case that one of these things becomes valuable *for me*. So suppose I feel somewhat pulled to get into soccer; I am enticed by the game, you might say, though I do not yet care about it in any meaningful way. Here I have a choice to make about whether this motive will be one that I affirm—a choice as to whether I will commit myself to caring about soccer. So when I give in to peer pressure and commit to trying to appreciate soccer as the beautiful game that my friends insist that it is, it seems that I *make* that activity valuable for me (or at least, a take an important first step toward that activity having value for me).[5] After all, in light of my decision, I now have (what I regard to be) weighty reasons to watch, learn about, discuss, and become emotionally vulnerable to soccer that I did not have prior to my endorsement

---

[5] For a full treatment of this process, see Callard 2018.

of that motive. Thus, my affirmation of soccer fandom is itself a key part of explaining why that activity now has value for me.

Perhaps we can read the Nietzschean as making a similar suggestion about how affirmation confers value. However, instead of focusing on a specific act that I might affirm (or not), the Nietzschean claim applies to one's life as a whole. On this view, then, I confer value on my life as a whole by affirming it. But though this interpretation seems sensible enough, I do not think it works for Nietzsche himself, who again, is famously skeptical of objective or categorical value.[6] After all, in the case at hand, the real work affirmation seems to do is to make it the case that something that independently has value (e.g., soccer) comes to have value for me. But of course, this is presupposing that the motive in question is connected to something that is valuable, or that my life, such as it is, is already valuable. And this presupposition is one that Nietzsche himself won't accept. Naturally, this doesn't mean that the above argument fails, but it does mean that it cannot be the reasoning that lies behind Nietzsche's high esteem for affirmation.

Yet even if Nietzsche could accept this argument, it is insufficient for the task at hand. For even if this argument is sound, it only shows that affirmation as such is required for meaning, but the Dionysian attitude involves more than *mere* affirmation. It requires the person in question to deliver a resounding yes to her life as a whole. One cannot halfheartedly affirm one's life, or pick and choose the aspects to affirm, or affirm it *on balance*. One must instead be so affirmatively "well disposed . . . to yourself and to life *to long for nothing more fervently* than for this ultimate eternal confirmation and seal" (Nietzsche 2001, §341). However, in the preceding example, nothing about my decision to embrace soccer rather than trying to become, say, a film buff or more knowledgeable about

---

[6] While everyone agrees that Nietzsche rejects objective or categorical values, the exact flavor of his metaethical commitments is a matter of significant controversy. For more, see Leiter 2015, Clark and Dudrick 2007, Hussain 2007, and Silk 2015.

wine requires my affirmation of the former motive to be so thoroughly wholehearted. The affirmation confers value for me because it is the result of *my* choice. And the choice is mine, not because I stand behind my choice in a final and unequivocal way, but simply because it was the result of an exercise of my normative competence. In other words, for the kind of *value-for-me* conferral that occurs in the sorts of cases described above, all that is required is that my affirmation be my own, and, as we saw in Chapter 3, all that *that* requires is that the decision (in this case, to affirm one motive rather than another) is caused by and reflects my capacities to recognize and respond to normatively significant considerations.

\*\*\*

Another possibility for why fervent or wholehearted affirmation is necessary for meaning starts from the thought that acts of human valuing are the *only* way value comes into being. And because wholehearted affirmation—a kind of affirmation that requires the agent's drives to be ordered in just the right way and for the agent to approve of that ordering—is the most robust way in which an agent can value something, it follows that to affirm your life in this way is maximally meaning-generating.

This strategy for defending the key premise in the Nietzschean Affirmation Argument more closely connects with Nietzsche's own axiological commitments (at least as Clark and Dudrick 2012 and Katsafanas 2016 unpack them). However, I think there are good reasons to think those axiological commitments are dubious. If there really is no value outside of human agents, how can our activities create it ex nihilo? This view seems to simply take as a brute fact that acts of human willing or valuing can create value where there was none prior to that activity. There must be, then, some basic or intrinsic goodness to the act of affirmation itself. But this is very puzzling: nothing is good except for human affirmation. I suppose that this sort of value chauvinism might be true, but I'm not sure why we should think that it is. After all, any argument that affirmation is intrinsically good is eo ipso an argument that there exists something with intrinsic value. But then, once we accept that there is something with intrinsic value, it's just not clear why we should doubt the existence of other instances of intrinsic value.

But supposing there is an answer to all this, or that I am badly mistaken in thinking through these axiological commitments, there still seems to be a deep problem with the idea that *only wholehearted affirmation* confers value or meaning. It is this. Meaningfulness is a scalar property. That is, agents' lives can be more or less meaningful. But whether an agent's affirmation of her life is wholehearted or not is not scalar. Either she affirms it wholeheartedly or she does not (either because she is ambivalent in her affirmation or because she does not affirm it at all). So even if it's correct that wholehearted affirmation is maximally value-conferring, it's not clear why less than wholehearted affirmation wouldn't at least confer some value to the agent. After all, if the demon's message is a test to evaluate whether one is a sheep or a goat, the person who is mostly exultant at the message—maybe she doesn't want to relive her time with her college boyfriend but is otherwise thrilled about the prospect of eternal recurrence—certainly seems more sheepish and less goatish than the person who is thoroughly horrified at the prospect of the demon's message being true. Thus even if wholehearted affirmation is the ideal—if that's the response to the demon's message that secures the *highest* kind of good life—it is nevertheless dubious that ambivalent affirmation gets you nothing of value.

If this response to the Nietzschean Affirmation Argument succeeds, it does not yet show that ambivalence as such isn't at odds with meaning. For that we must consider what it really means for an agent to affirm her life ambivalently. Without much consideration, you might think that this is at best an impoverished way of regarding one's life as a whole. That is, at first pass, it seems that the person who is halfhearted in her endorsement of how she has lived has, all things being equal, lived a much less rich or meaningful life than her wholehearted counterpart.

On reflection, however, I don't think this judgment is borne out. The fact that an ambivalent agent can still affirm her life despite failing to be unequivocally behind it reveals in her a level of commitment to her life that even the wholehearted agent lacks. After all, the wholehearted agent's innermost self is unified. And because there is no conflict, the demon's message would provide her with no threat of eternal loss. That is, because every action this agent has ever performed is one she wholeheartedly affirms, the prospect of eternal recurrence isn't one in which she would be forever separated from some aspect of who she is as an agent. This of course doesn't mean that it would be easy to wholeheartedly affirm one's life. But it does suggest that being wholehearted makes affirmation easier in this key respect.

For the ambivalent agent, though, if she does in fact affirm her life in the face of eternal recurrence, then she does so believing full well that by doing so she has to forever *give up* something that she identifies with. Here, one might think, the kind of commitment that it would take from an ambivalent agent to affirm her life should be *more* rather than less meaning-generating. That is, if we take the existentialist strand of thought running through this argument seriously, we should be more impressed with agents who, though deeply divided, resolve their wills and live their lives accordingly than we are by agents who, due entirely to luck or to an impoverished set of inner concerns, are never divided. If either of these is a higher type, worthy of admiration and emulation, it seems plausible that it is the former.

Thus, if affirmation is necessary to confer value or meaning, it is not clear why the affirmation in question must be fervent or wholehearted. Furthermore, it seems plausible that at least in certain cases, the kind affirmation that an ambivalent agent can achieve would confer more value for the agent. My choices mean more to me—they have more significance to me—when they cost me something. But precisely what I must do when I am ambivalent is choose in a way that results in value remainder. So the choices I make when

I am deeply torn over what to do matter more to me. And if the choice in question is whether or not to affirm the eternal recurrence of my life, then this seems all the more true. This Nietzschean interpretation of the key premise of the Affirmation Argument—that one must wholeheartedly affirm one's life as a whole in order to enjoy, as Clark (1990) puts it, the "ideal for human beings"—therefore fails.

## 4.5.2.  Why Affirmation Matters: Frankfurt's Story

As I understand Harry Frankfurt (particularly Frankfurt 2004), the fact that you would be willing to affirm your "volitional identity" is not what *makes* it the case that self-satisfaction is a valuable or meaningful state. And yet, if you are self-satisfied, you will finally and unequivocally affirm your inner self. So it is still true on Frankfurt's view that one enjoys the meaning-adjacent property of self-satisfaction only if one wholeheartedly affirms the inner elements of one's agency. And because you can only do that if those elements are unified—if they cohere and are well ordered—ambivalence will preclude you from being able to do this. Consequently, it also precludes the kind of meaningful contentment and satisfaction you might otherwise take in yourself.

But if by affirming her practical self an agent does not confer value or meaning on the subsequent state of being self-satisfied, what is the significance of affirmation here? On this point Frankfurt thinks that the agent's ability to affirm her practical self *reflects* or *manifests* her self-love. And *this* state, he tells us, is crucial for enjoying the most meaningful form of human agency. In other words, affirmation—the willingness on the part of the agent to "accept and endorse" her practical self—is itself the realization of the meaningful state. So while Frankfurt will accept the key claim in the Affirmation Argument, that you can enjoy the most meaningful form of human agency only if you are able to wholeheartedly affirm the innermost elements of your practical self, he thinks that this is true because the most meaningful form of human agency will manifest itself in wholehearted affirmation. On Frankfurt's view, then, the existence and value of self-love are prior to rather than dependent on the agent's willingness to affirm her practical self. The value of this sort of affirmation is therefore derived from the value of the state of self-love. So if we want to understand and assess why Frankfurt thinks wholehearted affirmation is valuable, we'll need to first understand why he thinks that self-love is valuable.

Frankfurt poses precisely this question as well. Indeed, he specifically asks, "Why should we think of self-love as desirable and important?" (2004, 96). In order to answer this question, however, it's important to remind ourselves of exactly how Frankfurt understands self-love. To do so, first recall that for Frankfurt, love is a disinterested concern for the welfare of the beloved. In the case of self-love, then, we have a disinterested concern for our own welfare. But what would it mean to have a disinterested concern for your own welfare? Among other things, it might entail wanting to be able to get what we want. But if so, then it'll be important that we do not impede that ability. Ambivalence does just this, since when we are ambivalent we experience a necessary inner conflict that cannot be resolved without remainder. That is, when we are ambivalent, then necessarily we'll be precluded from getting something that we want. A disinterested concern for my own welfare would therefore motivate me to become wholehearted, since in so doing I guarantee that I am no impediment to myself. It's for this reason that Frankfurt concludes that "to be wholehearted *is* to love oneself. The two are the same" (2004, 95).

This means that when Frankfurt asks about the value of self-love, he is, in essence, asking about the value of wholeheartedness itself, or as he subsequently puts it, "what is so wonderful about integrity and an undivided will" (2004, 96). In response to this question, he remarks:

One thing in favor of an undivided will is that divided wills are inherently self-defeating. Division of the will is a counterpart in the realm of conduct to self-contradiction in the realm of thought. A self-contradictory belief requires us, simultaneously, both to accept and to deny the same judgment. Thus is guarantees cognitive failure. Analogously, conflict within the will precludes behavioral effectiveness, by moving us in contrary directions at the same time. Deficiency in wholeheartedness is a kind of irrationality, then, which infects our practical lives and renders them incoherent.

By the same token, enjoying the inner harmony of an undivided will is tantamount to possessing a fundamental kind of freedom. Insofar as a person loves himself—in other words, to the extent he is volitionally wholehearted—he does not resist any movements of his will. He is not at odds with himself; he does not oppose, or seek to impede the expression in practical reasoning and in conduct whatever love his self-love entails. He is free in loving what he loves, at least in the sense that his loving is not obstructed or interfered with by himself.

Self-love has going for it, then, its role in constituting both the structure of volitional rationality and the mode of freedom that this structure of the will ensures. Loving ourselves is desirable and important for us because it is the same thing, more or less, as being satisfied with ourselves. (Frankfurt 2004, 96–97)

Self-love is thus valuable because it prevents us from practical self-defeat and in so doing it enables us to get what we really want the most. Given these values, it's no wonder that the wholehearted individual is happy to affirm her practical self. This is also why Frankfurt thinks that this kind of affirmation would be impossible for the person suffering from ambivalence.

The importance of affirmation, thus, derives from the fact that an agent's ability to "willingly accept and endorse [her] own volitional identity" (Frankfurt 2004, 97) reflects the high-water mark of well-functioning human agency. So although nothing about being ambivalent precludes you from getting much of what you want, on Frankfurt's view—you can get lucky and so come into lots of great things—the agent who loves herself, by contrast, even if she is terribly unlucky in achieving her goals, is nevertheless flawless with respect to the aspects of her life that are under her volitional control. And in assessing someone's agency, isn't *that* what matters?

Here, though, we might begin to wonder about just how plausible these claims really are. It's true that Frankfurt weaves a very tight web of conceptual connections between self-love, wholeheartedness, integrity, inner harmony, self-satisfaction, and endorsement or affirmation. And all of these things seem, in some way or other, to be attractive, desirable elements of a good, meaningful life. So if ambivalence threatens any one of them, as it clearly does with wholeheartedness, then it stands to reason that it must threaten them all. To fully evaluate the Frankfurtian version of the Affirmation Argument, then, we'll have to carefully access his claims that ambivalence guarantees self-defeat. I am much less sanguine than Frankfurt that it does. On the contrary, for reasons that I hope will soon be clear, I think that sometimes the only way to prevent self-defeat or self-betrayal is to maintain your ambivalence in the face of a terrible dilemma. However, a full appraisal of this argument requires more careful discussion of these issues. So for that reason, I'm going to set aside discussion of the Affirmation Argument (for now at least), and turn more directly to the argument that Frankfurt lays out here, the Argument from Self-Defeat.

# 5

# Ambivalence without Self-Defeat

## 5.1. The Problem of Integrity

The Resolution Argument fails to show that ambivalence undermines agents' autonomy. And so far, at least, we've seen that a Nietzschean version of the Affirmation Argument fails to show that ambivalent agents are unable to affirm their lives in a meaning-generating way. But in our exploration of the soundness of Frankfurt's version of the Affirmation Argument, it became clear that his defense of its key premise—that an agent can be satisfied and contented with herself only if she is able to fully accept and endorse her practical identity—merited more careful scrutiny. Indeed, the argument that Frankfurt marshals in support of his claims on that point can itself serve as a *direct* argument that ambivalence is a threat to the proper functioning of our wills, independently of its role in buttressing a key premise in the Affirmation Argument.

What Frankfurt offers us with this new argument, which I'll call the *Argument from Self-Defeat*, is an explanation for why wholeheartedness is necessarily preferable to ambivalence. It is, in other words, an account of why wholeheartedness is valuable in its own right and, correspondingly, why ambivalence as such is bad. More exactly, this argument purports to show that unless our practical self is unified, i.e., unless we are wholehearted in our willing, or unless we have "integrity" as agents, or unless we love ourselves, etc., we are at odds with ourselves in a necessarily self-defeating way. So insofar as we are ambivalent, we are an impediment to ourselves—specifically to our freedom to unequivocally pursue the things we

*In Praise of Ambivalence*. D. Justin Coates, Oxford University Press. © Oxford University Press 2023.
DOI: 10.1093/oso/9780197652398.003.0005

love. This means that insofar as we are ambivalent, we thereby guarantee self-defeat or even *self-betrayal*. It follows, then, that when we are ambivalent we lack integrity as agents. And because having the integrity to unabashedly pursue all and only that which you love is perhaps the best thing human agents can enjoy, ambivalence precludes well-functioning agency.

## 5.2. Self-Defeat as Self-Betrayal

Though I have so far been focused on Harry Frankfurt's development of these ideas, something like this general line of argument has in fact been the main historical source of unificationist worries about ambivalence. Indeed, it seems to be precisely what Plato was getting at when he claimed that "inner faction and not being of one mind" with ourselves "will make [us] incapable of action . . . it will make [us our] own enemy" (*Republic* 352a5). As Plato sees it, then, the ambivalent agent necessarily betrays herself and, as a result, lacks integrity. Christine M. Korsgaard takes up Plato's line of argument when she claims that in cases of unresolved agential conflict, "the deliberative procedures that [ideally] unify the soul into a single agent break down, and the person *as such* cannot act. . . . Platonic justice [i.e., agential integrity] is the constitutive principle of action" (2009, 152). This makes it seem that ambivalence is self-defeating because it precludes action altogether.

That ambivalence would preclude action in this way cannot literally be true. Ambivalent agents, after all, can be guided by reasons and comport their behavior in light of those considerations. What else would that be other than action? Moreover, they can make up their minds, resolve their practical questions, and even affirm their choices in just the ways that practical rationality demands. What they cannot do, of course, is any of these things wholeheartedly or without some significant internal division. So if Plato and Korsgaard are genuinely on to something here, as is reasonable to suppose, I do not think that the strongest version of the claims they make is credible. Perhaps a weaker version of what they claim is more defensible.

Just after claiming that a lack of justice (i.e., inner harmony, health of the soul, agential integrity, etc., etc.) makes us incapable of action—a claim too strong to be believable—Plato goes on to say of this sort of division that it "will make [us our] own enemy" (*Republic* 352a5). This suggests a weaker (and to my mind more plausible) gloss on his earlier claim that division makes us incapable of action. In particular, it suggests that when our souls are divided in some way, some element of our soul is usurping authority that (by Plato's lights) rightly belongs to the rational element of the soul. What this means is that when, say, a powerful appetitive desire masters our will, we are engaged in an act of *intra*soul treachery or betrayal. And while this does not prevent us from acting, it does mean that when we do act, we act without integrity.

This is perhaps clearest in the case of the kind of division that worries Plato and Korsgaard. Because they explicitly identify our rational capacities with the element of our souls that has final authority to direct our movements, it follows that any time we betray that element of ourselves and are moved by nonrational or irrational motives, we are necessarily acting against the seat of our principles—those commitments with which we are most fundamentally aligned. So while the agent experiencing inner faction can in fact act, she cannot act with integrity. Indeed, she is doubly lacking in integrity. First, she lacks psychological integrity: the elements of her soul are not properly integrated with one another. And second, she lacks normative integrity: she is not governed by her own principles. Inner faction therefore defeats us because it forces us to betray ourselves in these two ways.

This is a more plausible account of how a lack of unity is self-defeating than the literal one that Plato and Korsgaard apparently endorse. And yet it is not ultimately credible either. One problem stems from Plato's account of the soul and Korsgaard's acceptance and development of that view. For though it is no doubt true in some sense that we have rational, spirited, and appetitive motivations, these three allegedly independent sources of motivation are more closely connected than Plato imagines. My rational motives, for example, are not fully independent from my spirited or emotional engagement with the world. Indeed, it's at least in part because I am invested in and emotionally vulnerable to others that I have developed and am able to exercise rational executive control over my actions. Similarly, spirited motives—ones connected to emotions like shame or pride, to name but two examples—are quite intelligent or rational in ways that Plato fails to acknowledge. They are not merely the handmaids to the parts of our souls that are capable of highly abstract forms of rational contemplation, but are instead modalities by which I can come to understand and appreciate significant moral and rational truths. Indeed, it is regularly through these emotions that we are most closely in touch with normative reality. The idea, then, that there are three fully independent sources of motivation that compose us as agents does not withstand scrutiny.

But even setting these general worries about Plato's philosophical psychology aside, it's still not clear why the presence of inner faction necessarily involves self-betrayal and a worrisome lack of integrity. To briefly make the point—I'll come back to it in more detail below—think about political disagreement within a representational democracy. (I'm supposing here, *pace* Plato, that this is a just system of government.) In that context, legislators who represent people with different values and priorities disagree about not only what programs and goals are valuable, but also about how to correctly order their priorities. They have, in other words, disagreements that parallel the two types of ambivalence we discussed in Chapter 2: conflicts in identifying and conflicts in willing. In the case of the former type of conflict, there is perhaps no method of deliberation or debate that will fully convince a minority party that all of the things the majority party values are in fact valuable. But this does not mean that it is impossible to legitimately enact policies based on one of the values about which the legislative body is divided. The same is true when it comes to disagreements about how to prioritize the spending of tax revenues, since scarcity forces us to pick and choose which programs or goals we most value.

But supposing the majority party does not necessarily act illegitimately when it enacts policy proposals that the minority party disagrees with, we can ask ourselves, in what way is this legislative act self-defeating or one of self-betrayal? Setting aside the possibility that the *content* of the legislation is utterly antidemocratic (and here, I don't mean "undemocratic" in the loose or attenuated sense that appears often in sloppy political commentary, but a policy that, if enacted would materially destroy extant democratic institutions and replace them with antidemocratic ones), there is nothing self-defeating or self-betraying about such legislation *even though* it is not supported by a large group of citizens. In fact, we might think that this is good—not simply because we agree with the majority on the substance of their policy proposals—but because we think no other system of government is suitably responsive to the needs and preferences of its citizens, since to favor a system that secures maximal agreement between legislators is almost certainly one that does so by systematically giving no representation to some of its constituents' values and concerns. Rather than betraying the people they represent, the division that arises between these legislators accurately reflects divisions within the citizenry itself. There is thus a kind of honesty in the legislators' division that would be lacking if the legislature were composed in such a way as to wholly ignore the minority's values and priorities.

What this tells us is that self-betrayal is a more complicated thing than merely acting in a way that goes against some part of your practical self. Furthermore, it at least suggests—insofar as we want to follow Plato in trying to make claims about moral psychology on the basis of political theorizing—that ambivalence rather than wholeheartedness may be required for us to really have integrity. But as I say, this is, at best, "suggestive." In what follows, I'm going to return to Harry Frankfurt's more explicit development of self-defeat argument. And there I'll offer a more systematic defense of what I've only suggested so far: first, that ambivalence is not inherently self-defeating, second, that being wholehearted is sometimes an act of self-betrayal, and third, that as a result, ambivalence is sometimes the only option available to an agent who is interested in staying really true to who she is as an agent.

## 5.3. Frankfurt's Argument from Self-Defeat

As Frankfurt develops the Argument from Self-Defeat, it aims for its conclusion in two movements. First, he explains why ambivalence guarantees self-defeat. And second, he highlights what he takes to be the intrinsic badness of this state by comparing it to its more attractive counterpart: wholeheartedness. Thus for Frankfurt, the ambivalent agent is defective because the fragmentation of his will is necessarily self-defeating. Wholeheartedness, by contrast, is thought to secure meaningful forms of freedom and integrity. And, of course, when these valuable forms of freedom and integrity are present, we will happily affirm our practical selves. So his version of the argument (if sound) also provides us with grounds for accepting the Affirmation Argument.

As we've already seen, Frankfurt's argument that ambivalence is "inherently self-defeating" (2004, 96) relies on an analogy between ambivalence and self-contradictory belief. Just as believing and rejecting the same judgment leads to epistemic failure, he tells us that "conflict within the will precludes behavioral effectiveness, by moving us to act in contrary directions at the same time. Deficiency in wholeheartedness is a kind of irrationality, then, which infects our practical lives and renders them incoherent" (2004, 96). Frankfurt's contention, then, is simply that ambivalence, when its consequences are laid bare, is just as obviously a threat to the proper functioning of one's agency as accepting a self-contradiction is a threat to the proper functioning of one's doxastic capacities.

As stated, there are two reasons to think that these claims are mistaken. The first of these is that although a person can believe that p and also believe that ~p, it is not clear that it is actually possible to believe the conjunction of p and ~p. Indeed, I tend to think that it is fairly clear that it is *not* possible in standard cases.[1] So while Frankfurt is correct that believing the self-contradiction is inherently self-defeating, the set of explicitly self-contradictory beliefs is empty. He is making merely a conceptual claim that *if* you were to (impossibly) believe that (p & ~p), then you would guarantee that you had a false belief. But presumably, given how Frankfurt has conceptualized ambivalence here, he's not thinking that it's *merely* a conceptual claim that ambivalence is inherently self-defeating. Rather, he seems committed to thinking that actual agents can and do experience ambivalence with some regularity. What this means, however, is that by Frankfurt's own lights, the analogy is one that we should be suspicious of, since the state to which ambivalence is being compared isn't one that human agents can be in.

If we are going to learn something from Frankfurt's analogy, then I propose that we alter it slightly. Ambivalence, if it is comparable to doxastic states, is perhaps more closely comparable to the state of being such that you believe that p and also that you believe that ~p. If each of these beliefs is in your set of beliefs, then it follows that that set is incoherent. And so we could conclude that ambivalence similarly involves volitional incoherence on the part of the agent. But notice that although there is something to this bit of analogical reasoning, it's much harder to get to the sweeping conclusion that Frankfurt arrives at. The reason for this is that although

---

[1] By way of "argument" for this claim, I invite you to attempt to *believe* that <Julius Caesar was taller than two meters and it's not the case that Julius Caesar was taller than two meters>.

an incoherent set of beliefs affects an agent's ability to believe all and only true things, it does not necessarily preclude cognitive effectiveness. After all, each of us *actually* has an incoherent set of beliefs. Indeed, *no* human agent has ever managed to avoid this. And yet, for all of our doxastic incoherence, we are still able to enjoy a high degree of cognitive effectiveness. So if we want to accept Frankfurt's analogy here, we must dial back its upshot. If doxastic incoherence does not preclude cognitive effectiveness, we should not think—at least on the basis of Frankfurt's analogy—that ambivalence precludes behavioral effectiveness either. In other words, we cannot, on the basis of its similarities to having an incoherent set of beliefs, conclude that ambivalence is inherently self-defeating.

Of course, even if one accepts that just as no single instance of incoherent beliefs will destroy an agent's cognitive capacities, no individual instance of ambivalence is itself self-defeating in a way that is sufficient to radically undermine freedom or integrity, the unificationists still have one last card to play. It is this. If my set of beliefs is sufficiently incoherent—if say, for *any* belief that I have, I also believe its negation, or for any proposition to which I assign a high credence, I am happy to assign a high credence to its negation—then it seems I would be cognitively deficient in a significant way. And this will hold even if my incoherence is not so extreme. From this, we might also worry that a sufficiently robust *pattern* of ambivalence—a regular or frequent inability to settle your will—does seem like it might threaten your ability to live your life in the way you see fit. This is intrinsically bad, but it's also bad for another reason, which is that you might think that this ability is (in part) constitutive of a well-lived life for creatures like us.[2]

---

[2] Of course, if you're really ambivalent, then it's not clear that you'll have a settled conception of a good life in the first place. This is because ambivalence involves fragmentation at the deepest levels of an agent's practical identity—the precise aspects of our practical identities that Frankfurt takes to constitute our conception of a good life. Indeed, according to Frankfurt (2004), you cannot determine what constitutes a good life without first determining what you love. But if you are ambivalent about what you love, then it might seem that you cannot have a settled conception of what a good life

If it is bad to be such that you are unable to freely pursue those ends you identify with, as is the case with the regularly ambivalent agent, then a natural follow-up question comes to mind: what could correct this? The answer, of course, is wholeheartedness, since it secures for the agent a will that is free from fragmentation, a will that puts no obstacles before the agent that might compromise her integrity. As Frankfurt puts it:

> By the same token, *enjoying the inner harmony of an undivided will is tantamount to possessing a fundamental kind of freedom.* Insofar as a person loves himself—in other words, to the extent he is volitionally wholehearted—he does not resist any movements of his will. *He is not at odds with himself;* he does not oppose, or seek to impede, the expression in practical reasoning and in con- duct of whatever love his self-love entails. He is free in loving what he loves, at least in the sense that his loving is not obstructed or interfered with by himself. (2004, 97; emphasis added)

Wholeheartedness, and with it self-love (and affirmation), is the cure to ambivalence's ills. It enables, rather than detracts from, be- havioral effectiveness. So whereas the regularly ambivalent agent defeats herself, the wholehearted agent enhances his own agency and the satisfaction he can take in its exercise. Wholeheartedness is, for Frankfurt, the only way to save yourself from your self.

The forcefulness of this version of Frankfurt's Argument from Self-Defeat notwithstanding, I'm not sanguine that even this tempered and more careful version of the argument succeeds in showing that (i) a pattern of ambivalence defeats one's practical self in just the way that a pattern of doxastic incoherence defeat one's epistemic self, and (ii) that wholeheartedness, because it is a

---

would be for you. It is therefore no wonder that Frankfurt claims that, wherever possible, ambivalence should be excised from our wills, or at least, it should be managed the way one might manage a long-term illness.

form of freedom from inner turmoil, is necessarily a good thing. In the remainder of this chapter, then, I consider more carefully the analogy that Frankfurt utilizes. Even if we set aside the more formal worries I've already expressed about it, it's doubtful that it can secure his conclusions. To the contrary, I contend that wholeheartedness does not necessarily secure freedom or integrity. There are cases in which agents must be ambivalent in order to maintain their integrity as agents, in order to prevent self-betrayal. The necessary connections between wholeheartedness, self-love, affirmation, and satisfaction are thus illusory.

## 5.4. Is Ambivalence Necessarily Self-Defeating?

To begin, I want to first consider a simple argument that ambivalence is not self-defeating. This argument is sound, but unfortunately, it is not (quite) germane to Frankfurt's overall argumentative strategy. Despite this, it does illuminate something important.

Anti-Self-Defeat Argument
1. If ambivalence is necessarily self-defeating, then it always leaves the ambivalent agent worse off.
2. There are cases in which an ambivalent agent is better off than she would have been had she been wholehearted.
3. So ambivalence is not necessarily self-defeating.

This argument clearly rests on the claim that there are cases in which ambivalence leaves agents better off than wholeheartedness would. One general kind of example of this sort of phenomenon occurs in cases in which, owing to her ambivalence, a person does not "rush into" big decisions and so is less prone to the kinds of calamities that often occur when the sorts of actions that people wholeheartedly rush into go awry.[3] Indeed, I know this all too well: I have been wholehearted in some of my worst decisions. Had my will been divided, then although I might have still ended up making many of the same terrible decisions, I probably would have done so with more caution and only after having given more careful thought to exit strategies. As a result, it's plausible that I could have avoided some of the more disastrous consequences those decisions had in my own life and in the lives of those I care about. The fact that I would have been less "free" in the sense of freedom allegedly secured by wholeheartedness or had less integrity seems a small price to pay in overall evaluations of the overall value of those actions for me and for those that were affected by them.

But though this argument provides us with some reason to value ambivalence, it is ultimately orthogonal to Frankfurt's Argument from Self-Defeat. At its core, Frankfurt's attack on ambivalence isn't actually relying on the idea that if we are wholehearted, our lives will be better off in material ways. This might be generally true, of course, but in fact Frankfurt (1999, 2004) himself concedes that ambivalence can have positive instrumental value in some (perhaps many) cases. Indeed, in such cases, it might therefore be all-things-considered rational for agents to be ambivalent. So Frankfurt is aware, to some degree, that ambivalence is not necessarily self-defeating in the sense that it always leaves the ambivalent agent worse off. What this means is that we need to correctly identify the scope of Frankfurt's key claims. In particular, I think we should understand unificationists like Frankfurt as making a direct argument that our *agency as such* is somehow threatened by ambivalence, even if that threat is not one that leaves the agent herself

---

[3] Of course, you might worry that an ambivalent agent will drag her feet in a way that makes her worse off. This is no problem for what I say here, however, since all I want to do is note that ambivalence can have value for an agent, but this is consistent with ambivalence being disvaluable for agents in some circumstances (though insofar as ambivalence can be bad for someone, it is not because it represents a failure in the structure of her will). In so doing, I ally myself with Susan Wolf (2002) and Jacqui Poltera (2011), who each explicitly note this in their discussions of the value of ambivalence.

worse off. Accordingly, the real heart of Frankfurt's argument that ambivalence is inherently self-defeating must ultimately begin (and end) with his claim that a divided will is analogous to incoherence in the realm of thought, since although incoherence is sometimes instrumentally neutral or even good, it is always intrinsically bad.

So: is it really the case that ambivalence in the will is analogous to doxastic incoherence? No doubt, when an agent is divided the agent lacks a kind of internal harmony that many of us prize. Surely, however, finding yourself in a situation in which, given facts about the volitions that constitute your practical identity, there are two divergent courses of action that are each independently worth pursuing is *very* different from believing a self-contradictory proposition to be true. For one thing, setting issues related to dialetheism aside, most of us think that if an agent were to believe the conjunction of p and ~p, she would believe something that is *necessarily* false. After all, given certain plausible assumptions (e.g., the principle of bivalence), at most p or ~p (but not both) can be true. So the belief that (p & ~p) cannot possibly turn out to be true. Now, as I already said, I don't think self-contradictory belief can be what's doing the work in Frankfurt's argument, but we don't need anyone to be able to believe a self-contradictory claim in order to generate doxastic incoherence. For it's also true that if I believe that p and I also believe that ~p—say, because in one domain, considerations that p plausible seem salient, while in another, independent domain, considerations that ~p seem salient—then on the assumptions spelled out above, it is necessarily true that I have a false belief.

However, is the same thing true in the practical domain? When confronted with a choice between either *a*-ing and ~*a*-ing, an agent might be ambivalent as to which motive she should act on. But her regarding *a*-ing and ~*a*-ing to be choiceworthy, perhaps equally so, and being torn between *a*-ing or ~*a*-ing even though it is impossible to both *a* and ~*a*, is hardly the same as believing p & believing ~p. One plausible explanation for this, I think, is simply that our beliefs aim to represent the world as it is, and the world cannot be accurately represented as somehow conflicting with itself—unicorns cannot exist and not exist, for example. As a result, the possession of two beliefs that represent the world in this way will necessarily lead to an inaccurate representation of the world. However, the logic of desiderative states (or of conation more generally) is not like this. We have incompatible desires when we desire $a$-ing and $\sim a$-ing simultaneously, but the incoherence here seems innocent. Consider: what criticism can you level against the agent who right now wants to go to the ice cream parlor and also, right now, wants to go to the park? You can tell her, "We can't do both right now" and invite her to prioritize her preferences, of course. But the charge of desiderative *irrationality* does not seem apt, or even sensible as an objection you could make of the set of a person's desires.

Unlike the agent who believes that p and believes that $\sim$p, and in so doing is irrational, the person who wants to go to the ice cream parlor at $t_1$ and also not go to the ice cream parlor at $t_1$ (because she wants to go to the park at $t_1$) seems merely unlucky that the ice cream parlor isn't at the park. No doubt, one of her desires must go unrealized in this case, but whatever "badness" we want to attach to having an unrealized desire as such, it is hardly comparable to the badness of theoretical irrationality. More generally, this points us toward a key way in which the axiological world is systematically different from the alethic one. There is only one way the world *is*. But there are many things that are fit for our wanting, or caring about, or loving. As a result, we should not expect psychological states that are at least somewhat connected to agents' conception of the good (desires, cares, loves, values, etc.) to be subject to the kind of demands for coherence that alethic states are.[4]

---

[4] I say "somewhat connected" because I do not mean to take a stand on debates about the "guise of the good" here. Nor do I mean to suggest that what one cares about, for example, necessarily rests on or reflects what one judges to be good—indeed many care theorists deny precisely this. But even if it is possible to care about something without holding it to be good in any way, surely there are typically causal connections between

Of course, one crucial exception to this claim is intention. As Michael Bratman (1984) has argued, intentions must be *strongly consistent* relative to our beliefs, where this means that if I intend to *a* and I believe that *a* is not possible, then I am irrational.[5] Here the charge of irrationality has more bite, and so perhaps Frankfurt's worry about the fragmentation that occurs in an ambivalent agent's will is on a par with *this* variety of practical irrationality. After all, if a person intends to go to the ice cream parlor right now and also intends to go to the park right now, and she knows that it's not possible to do both, she seems irrational. That is, her intentions are not just incompatible, as is the case with her desires; they are also the source of a particularly objectionable form of incoherence or irrationality. And this kind of mistake really does look very much like it is of a piece with the mistake one makes when you believe that p and also believe that ~p. So if this is the mistake that's cooked into ambivalence, then Frankfurt's argument has significant force indeed.

But do ambivalent agents violate the demands of strong consistency that govern intentions? Maybe they do in some cases, of course. But it's actually fairly clear that an ambivalent agent does not fail to be strongly consistent, *merely in virtue of her ambivalence*. The reason for this is that neither the account of ambivalence that Frankfurt offers nor the one that I developed earlier (which supplements Frankfurt's in some key ways) requires that the ambivalent agent *intend* to act on each of the inner motives that pull her in incompatible directions. What ambivalence requires instead is that an agent is genuinely motivated by psychological states that are part of her innermost practical self to act in distinct yet

---

the things we regard as important and valuable and the things we care about. Even this minimal kind of connection is sufficient for what I want to claim here.

[5] Bratman is actually explicit in claiming that desires are not required to be consistent in this way. He writes: "I might, without irrationality, both desire to play basketball today and desire to finish this paper today, all the time knowing I cannot do both" (1984, 380–81).

incompatible ways. But of course, this is consistent with the agent intending only to act on one of those motives when the time for acting finally arrives. Thus there is nothing about ambivalence per se that guarantees this kind of irrationality.

If ambivalence does not involve this sort of irrationality, and instead only involves the kind of conflict between desiderative states (and the like), then we do not need to be too worried by Frankfurt's analogy. The conflicts that occur between our innermost motives are undoubtedly genuine conflicts, but they are not therefore open to formal objections of the sort that charges of irrationality or incoherence tend to amount to. There might nevertheless be criticisms we can make of agents who experience ambivalence—maybe there are decisive grounds not to care about one of the sources of the conflict, either because the object of care is not objectively worthy of the agent's concern or because it is not consistent with more basic motivational commitments of the agent. But these criticisms take as their object the substance of what the ambivalent agent wants or loves or cares about or values. Such criticisms might often be correct, and so there might be good grounds for criticizing individuals who are ambivalent when they should not be. Perhaps it's even true that in some cases in which agents are ambivalent though they should not be, their ambivalence ultimately is self-defeating.

However, let's note that this version of an argument from self-defeat is decidedly different from the one that Frankfurt is pushing, since this argument's conclusion is that it is, at most, ambivalence with respect to things one should not be ambivalent about that is self-defeating. In other cases of ambivalence, cases in which the motives that come in to conflict are each responsive to something that is genuinely worthy of the agent's concern, there is nothing that is obviously irrational about her ambivalence. In fact, if we accept even a minimal form of pluralism, which allows that many states of affairs can have something going for them, such that they are worthy of our care and attention, then an agent's ambivalence actually looks like *it*, rather than wholeheartedness, might be what rationality demands, given the agent's concerns. The kind of conflict involved in ambivalence, in other words, can be a conflict that arises not because the agent is irrational but precisely because she is responding to a difficult truth: there is much in the world worth wanting, but, alas, we cannot have it all. In other words, it seems that an ambivalent agent might be responding exactly as a well-functioning agent would.[6]

This points us toward an even deeper difference between the theoretical and practical realms in this respect—viz., that whereas believing p and believing ~p is sure to guarantee self-defeat in one's cognitive faculties, being torn between $a$-ing and $~a$-ing is *sometimes necessary for practical success*. That is, in some circumstances, it seems that we are well functioning as agents *only if* we are ambivalent. In many cases of practical conflict—for example, those of the sort that Erica finds herself in—an agent who fails to be torn between the alternatives will, necessarily, be an agent who fails to take seriously the value residue that would result from either of her decisions. But surely well-functioning agency requires this of us.

So much for the idea that ambivalence is inherently self-defeating. But even if it is not, there is a second move in Frankfurt's argumentative strategy, which is a direct argument that wholeheartedness is necessary for well-functioning agency. This is the subject of Chapter 6, where we'll see not only that wholeheartedness does not necessarily secure freedom or integrity, but that to get these goods, an agent might in fact need to be ambivalent. But before turning to that iteration of the Argument from Self-Defeat, I want to return to the unfinished business from the previous chapter, which concerns Frankfurt's version of the Affirmation Argument.

---

[6] I take up this point in much more detail in Chapter 8.

## 5.5. Affirmation Revisited

Recall that for Frankfurt, an agent's willingness to affirm her volitional identity manifested both her self-love and a fulfilling form of
self-satisfaction that is, although not sufficient for a good life, certainly a key component of many well-lived lives. It was in the context of expounding on this point that Frankfurt offers the Argument
from Self-Defeat. Specifically, he claims that the reason an ambivalent agent cannot affirm her volitional identity is because her ambivalence guarantees behavioral ineffectiveness, and it so doing, it
is inherently self-defeating. And who could genuinely affirm her
practical commitments when those very practical commitments
were the source of her undoing?

We now see that this line of argument fails. Ambivalence is
not inherently self-defeating. Frankfurt's argument for this claim
rests on an illicit comparison between ambivalence and self-
contradictory belief. But beyond even the failure of his analogy,
Frankfurt's general strategy suffers in that it fails to recognize that
there are many things that are worthy of the concern we pour into
them. That the world does not arrange itself in a way that allows us
to pursue and realize and enjoy *all* of our hearts' desires in no way
obviates this truth.

What does this mean for affirmation? First, it suggests that affirmation need not be the manifestation of self-love, where this
is simply understood as wholeheartedness. The reason for this is
simply that an ambivalent agent, even if she is disappointed that
she will not be able to do justice to two of the motives that define
her agency, might nevertheless regard her commitment to each
of those motives as absolutely essential for her practical identity.
Her ability to affirm her volitional identity is, as Frankfurt says of
the wholehearted agent, no less important for her self-satisfaction
than it would be if her volitional commitments were unified. What
this means is that Frankfurt is right that affirmation manifests a
meaning-adjacent good—an ability to affirm and take satisfaction

in one's practical commitments is deeply intertwined with living well—but he is mistaken in thinking it possesses these virtues because it issues from a wholehearted will. So here, again, we see, as we did with Nietzsche, not a complete mistake on the unificationists' part—that I can affirm my life as a whole or my practical self in response to the demon's message is indeed important. But nothing is added by wholeheartedness, and the fact that an agent is ambivalent when she affirms her life/agency might actually enhance the significance of that affirmation.

## 5.6. Conclusion

At this point, we've seen how the first movement of Frankfurt's Argument from Self-Defeat fails to show that ambivalence is inherently self-defeating. We've also seen, in brief, why it is that ambivalence might actually be necessary if one wants to avoid betraying one's innermost commitments or values in cases of practical conflict. In other words, what we've really seen is how ambivalence rather than wholeheartedness might be necessary for an agent facing conflict to maintain her *integrity*.[7] But this last point deserves more careful attention and scrutiny. If ambivalence proves to be valuable in the face of certain kinds of practical conflicts and dilemmas, then we'll have reason to reject the second movement of Frankfurt's Argument from Self-Defeat, which holds that only wholeheartedness can secure an especially valuable form of freedom and agential integrity.

To develop this point, I want to consider in some detail the conflict at the center of Aeschylus's tragedy *Agamemnon*. In that tale, an agent finds himself in precisely the sort of practical conflict that I regard as rationalizing ambivalence rather than wholeheartedness. And as we'll see, his mistake wasn't necessarily the choice

---

[7] Here I follow Calhoun (1995).

he makes, but how his will came to be structured in making that choice. Specifically, he makes himself wholehearted in Frankfurt's sense and is worse off qua agent for it. For agents in situations like Agamemnon's, we'll see, genuine integrity and freedom from self-betrayal only come with ambivalence.

# 6

# Ambivalence and Integrity

## 6.1. Trouble in Aulis

In Aeschylus's (1984) *Agamemnon* the eponymous character is
put to an awful test. As the king of the Achaeans, Agamemnon is
charged with upholding and defending Zeus's exacting standards
of justice and hospitality. This means that when Paris, a Trojan
prince, violates the Achaeans' goodwill and hospitality by running
off with Agamemnon's sister-in-law—a grave affront to both family
and state—Agamemnon seemingly has no choice but to lead the
Achaeans to war.

Unfortunately for Agamemnon, the goddess Artemis has promised to stay the winds and thereby prevent his warships from
launching if he is unable to provide an adequate sacrifice. And even
worse for Agamemnon, it turns out that the only sacrifice that she
is willing to accept is the life of his daughter Iphigenia. He is thus
faced with an extremely difficult choice—perhaps even an impossible choice, since neither course of action is one that, ex ante,
Agamemnon could anticipate as being able to *live with*. On the one
hand, if he opts for sparing his daughter, the war effort will fail. So
too, he would fail as the Achaean king, since he is the one charged
with upholding Zeus's demands. He would also fail as a brother,
since the bonds of family require that he not allow his brother
Menelaus's humiliation to go unavenged. On the other hand,
if he instead chooses to kill Iphigenia, he will fail in others ways.
Obviously, he would fail Iphigenia, whom he loves. But he would

*In Praise of Ambivalence*. D. Justin Coates, Oxford University Press. © Oxford University Press 2023.
DOI: 10.1093/oso/9780197652398.003.0006

also fail himself, since the genuine love and affection he feels for his daughter is also deeply integrated into who Agamemnon is as an individual. It is within these constraints that Agamemnon must make his decision.

However, as it happens—at least in Aeschylus's retelling of the tale—this extremely difficult choice doesn't actually take very long. After a brief display of anguish, Agamemnon decides that he must kill Iphigenia. But unlike in the case of the patriarch Abraham, who is also said to have found himself in similarly troubling circumstances, Providence is unkind to Agamemnon, and no sacrificial ram appears in Aulis, as it did on the mountain; no one appears to prevent Agamemnon's sacrifice.[1] Agamemnon thus carries out the horrific act, becoming his own daughter's executioner.

Yet as tragic as Agamemnon's situation appears, you might worry that it cannot generalize to the sorts of conflicts actual agents are faced with in a way that is philosophically interesting. After all, the dilemma that Agamemnon faces at Aulis is one that is, in some crucial respects, almost completely foreign to us as modern readers. The idea, for example, that doing justice requires exacting bloody vengeance against those who violate hospitality standards seems quite strange, to say the least. And this strangeness is not, I think, due to the fact that we are simply happy to accept insults. Even modern readers can imagine being upset in the way that Menelaus would have been upset when he discovers that Paris has seduced and abducted his wife. Rather, what's strange, I submit, is the apparent deontic necessity that Agamemnon and his followers attach to their response: it is a genuine *imperative*. In other words, for Agamemnon and for the other Achaeans, letting the Trojans' insult pass without violent retribution would have been genuinely *unthinkable*. But for many of us, this is not the case. We haven't lost the desire for meeting wrongdoing and grave insults with retaliatory

---

[1] See Genesis 22:1–14.

violence, but we have cultivated the ability to consider nonviolent alternatives.[2]

Even more foreign, however, is the idea that the demands of hospitality in particular could be so strong as to oblige one to sacrifice a beloved child. Indeed, it is very hard to imagine, even for the purposes of purely abstract philosophical speculation, circumstances in which killing a beloved child seems reasonable or even genuinely *doable*. But even if there is some "ticking time bomb" case that will suffice, surely Agamemnon's willingness to treat the demands of hospitality as being so important that they rationalize his killing of Iphigenia is itself utterly bizarre, at least from our modern perspective. Perhaps *some*thing could justify her sacrifice, but not *that*. Agamemnon thus faces a dilemma that is barely comprehensible to us, given how we live.

But though the sources of Agamemnon's dilemma are foreign to us today, this does not mean that we should simply ignore the plight that he faces. Even if the particular dilemma that Agamemnon finds himself facing is not one that we can really envision ourselves confronting—after all, I'll never be king, I'll never interact with real gods, I'll never value hospitality in the way that ancient Achaeans did, etc.—the dilemma Agamemnon faces nevertheless exhibits a choice structure with which we are intimately familiar. We can see this by considering difficult but utterly banal practical dilemmas of the sort that we often confront in our own lives.

Consider again Erica's dilemma. Now, if professional prestige and money mean nothing to Erica, then there's no real dilemma— she'll simply refuse the job and stay where she is able to continue caring for her parents. So too, if she doesn't really care about her

---

[2] Some modern readers might find a desire for retaliatory violence to be morally appalling. Perhaps it is, but I'm more doubtful that this is the case. To the contrary, it's plausible that the presence of the desire in question (or some similarly *untamed*, *uncivilized* desire) is itself a response to the fact that a real social good—something like the good of *honor*—is threatened by actions like those of Paris. (And of course this is consistent with thinking one shouldn't act on such a desire for a variety of reasons.) For more, see Sommers 2018.

parents' welfare and has just been taking care of them because no ready excuse not to has provided itself, then no dilemma arises. The existence of a genuine dilemma, rather than a mere choice between competing options, depends on the options bringing central elements of an individual's practical identity into conflict.[3] It's because Erica cares deeply about professional success *and* also loves her parents very much that the job offer presents, in this case, a difficult choice for her. And this is precisely what is at stake for Agamemnon: his love for kingdom and for his brother's honor on the one hand and his love for his daughter on the other are, tragically, at odds with one another.

So although we can no longer identify with the specific motives and practical commitments that lead to Agamemnon's personal dilemma, our lives are filled with situations in which our motives and our practical commitments have put us into structurally isomorphic, if perhaps lower-stakes, dilemmas. There is great value, then, in better appreciating Agamemnon's dilemma, foreign though it might seem, since it is by understanding how Agamemnon's dilemma arises, and more importantly, how it should be resolved, that we can better understand what exactly well-functioning agency demands of us when we find ourselves confronted with dilemmas of our own. We thus have reason to carefully reflect on the foreign world of the ancient Achaeans. We might not be at home there, but even so, there is a great deal that we can learn from Aeschylus, and from the tragic figure at the center of his story.

---

[3] As I understand "difficult dilemmas" or "hard choices" in this passage, the difficulty is one that emerges from the fact that each option seems attractive to the agent because motives that are internal to her practical self commend it to her. This is a way of understanding the notion of difficulty or "hardness," as it is relevant to resolving practical conflicts, different from the one Ruth Chang (2017) has recently introduced. According to Chang, hard choices are hard because the options are on a par. She's right, of course, that this is one thing that can make a choice hard, but as we see in Agamemnon's case, which doesn't involve parity, surely it is not the *only* thing.

## 6.2. Agamemnon's Wholeheartedness

Despite the psychological difficulty of Agamemnon's choice, Aeschylus presents it as, in some sense, the only choice that is open to him. We are told, for instance, that Agamemnon "slipped his neck in the strap of Fate" (Aeschylus 218). This has led many to read Aeschylus as claiming that Agamemnon is fated to perform the action by supernatural forces that are wholly outside of his control. And if so, then Agamemnon looks less like an agent we might learn something from than like a divine puppet. To the contrary, Bernard Williams has forcefully argued that this interpretation of Agamemnon's agency "simply misrepresents the text" (1993, 133). The "strap of fate" that Agamemnon bears is one that *he* slips his neck into. What this means, Williams concludes, is that if it is necessary that Agamemnon do what he does, then it is Agamemnon who *makes* it necessary. But how can this be? How can Agamemnon be the one who makes his choice "fated" or necessary?

To answer these questions, we must carefully attend to the fact that the real source of Agamemnon's dilemma is not external to his practical commitments. Rather, the dilemma arises because of his own commitment to, on the one hand, his kingdom, and on the other, his daughter. It is, of course, tragic that the world ended up being a place in which these commitments are at odds with one another, such that Agamemnon cannot properly honor both commitments. But we shouldn't thereby conclude that the dilemma itself arises simply as a result of how events unfolded in the world. Agamemnon's choice is not the workings of "fate" because the world makes it so. It is "fated" because, as Heraclitus says, "a man's character is his fate" (Williams 1993, 136). If Agamemnon had not cared about the demands of kingship, or brotherhood, or honor, then he'd have little motivation to pursue Paris back to Troy, and so he'd have little reason to be concerned with Athena's threats. Or if Agamemnon had not cared about Iphigenia, then he'd find the prospect of her sacrifice an inconvenience at worst. What this means is that Agamemnon faces his fateful choice precisely because of who he is as an agent, because of his innermost practical self.

However, it's worth noting here that this only shows, at most, that given his particular psychological profile, Agamemnon *must* choose one way or the other—not that the particular choice he makes is necessary. Yet when one reads Aeschylus, it's hard not to think that it *is* in some sense necessary that Agamemnon kill Iphigenia. What could be the source of this necessity?

Remarking on just this point, Martha Nussbaum (2001) claims that it is *rational* necessity and not some externally located causal necessity that binds Agamemnon's choice. As she puts it, "The choice to sacrifice Iphigenia . . . seems clearly preferable, both because of the consequences and because of the impiety involved in the other choice. Indeed, it is hard to imagine that Agamemnon could rationally have chosen any other way" (2001, 34). If Nussbaum is correct about this, it means that when Aeschylus talks of Agamemnon slipping his neck into the strap of fate, he's not just being absolved of all agency or responsibility. Rather, it's Aeschylus's way of showing that Agamemnon is shouldering the painful burden that he must in light of his character—at least if he is to remain a recognizably rational agent. This, in turn, means that not only does Aeschylus see the decision to sacrifice Iphigenia as rationally required, but that we should as well.

But is it really the case that Agamemnon could not have rationally decided to refuse to go through with Iphigenia's sacrifice, that, in the circumstances, the only rational course of action for him was to kill his own daughter? This is a striking claim, and at first glance it's not clear that it's true. After all, it's quite easy to imagine his love for his daughter being so great that he would not sacrifice her for *anything*. Indeed, it's even possible that such an action really would be genuinely unthinkable for him. In such a case, the fact that it would be impossible for Agamemnon to execute Iphigenia would have its source not from external forces that apparently constrain his options but in the (imagined) structure of Agamemnon's will.

But even if this were true of Agamemnon, then although it would certainly be *understandable* that Agamemnon chooses to spare her, it's not altogether clear that this would suffice to make it rational for him to do so.[4] It might very well do so, of course, but let's note also that this is just the sort of case that invites invocations of clichés. In this case, it would seem that Agamemnon's love for Iphigenia has blinded him to other sources of value. Yet when we seek to explain someone's behavior by invoking the idea that "love is blind," we are providing grounds for understanding what someone is doing, but we are in no way defending the rationality of doing it.

Accordingly, I think Nussbaum is basically right: the comparative gains and losses are simply too much in favor of sacrificing Iphigenia. Moreover, she will almost certainly die in either case, so in all likelihood, all Agamemnon would do by sparing her would be to keep himself from being directly responsible for her death. And the value of having one's hands clean, such as it is, surely doesn't outweigh the value of the lives of so many other persons.

These facts, of course, don't mean that his choice is easy. In fact, it's not one that I think that *I* could make—at least, given my current perspective on the world, I can't see how to get to *that* decision. However, Agamemnon—at least as he's described in Aeschylus, Homer, and elsewhere—surely values the standards of honor with which a king must conduct himself much more than I do, so he has perhaps less ground to travel. I also suspect that he values Iphigenia much less than I value my daughters, since I think that the attitudes I have toward them are ones that many men (particularly powerful men like Agamemnon) came to see as fitting only relatively recently. But despite this, I'm not sure that even these differences between Agamemnon and contemporary parents would be enough to make the choice to spare one's child an all-things-considered

---

[4] That it might be rational for Agamemnon to refrain from killing Iphigenia is easy to make sense of on at least some theories of practical rationality. If what he cares most deeply about is her welfare, then on some Humean theories, it'll turn out that he has especially weighty reasons to spare her. See, e.g., Frankfurt 1982 and Goldman 2009.

rational one.[5] Certainly, from Agamemnon's point of view it could not have made sense to simply ignore the standards of hospitality and honor that he identified with or to ignore the ruin that would come to the Greeks if he failed to meet these standards. The necessity, then, wasn't just that he had no desirable options, as Nussbaum suggests; it was also that *given his own values and commitments*, he had to choose a course of action that in almost any other context would not have even occurred to him.

Consequently, the interesting philosophical or existential question is *not* primarily the question whether Agamemnon should have refrained from killing his daughter, since it is plausible that was the best thing to do in the circumstances.[6] Instead, the real question is something along the following lines: how should Agamemnon, and by extension those of us who bear witness to his tragic choice, understand and respond to the decision itself? Taking up this question, Nussbaum herself suggests that for Agamemnon "both courses [of action] involve him in guilt" (2001, 34). If this is correct, then it seems that no matter how he chooses, Agamemnon must recognize and deal with the fact that he has acted wrongly and that he is responsible for his act of wrongdoing. That is, Agamemnon cannot take himself to be justified in killing Iphigenia simply because her sacrifice was the only course of action that was rationally open to him.

Of course, Nussbaum's claim, which assumes that there are genuine tragic moral dilemmas in which agents will act *wrongly* no matter what they do, is quite controversial. Some might reasonably

---

[5] Maybe this merely tells us something significant about how unimportant being all-things-considered rational is to living a good life.

[6] For everything I've said here, one might still insist, as G. E. M. Anscombe (1958) does, that even *considering* the possibility of killing an innocent person reveals a corrupt mind. Perhaps this is correct, but it's also a kind of high-mindedness that would have offered no help for Agamemnon, who will either be responsible for the death of his innocent daughter directly or the destruction of his kingdom and deaths of his people indirectly. The fact that he would not intend the latter outcome would not absolve him of blame, since one need not intentionally cause a state of affairs to come about in order to be morally responsible for it.

argue that if Agamemnon genuinely lacks rational alternatives, then he is in fact justified in sacrificing his daughter (see Conee 1982). However, if Agamemnon is rationally justified in so acting (as Nussbaum accepts), then it's hard to see how he could be genuinely blameworthy for his actions. After all, we typically think that an agent cannot be blameworthy for what she did if what she did wasn't wrong.

But even supposing that this is correct, and that Agamemnon is *not* blameworthy for the death of his daughter, it doesn't follow that all is well in Aulis. Even if Agamemnon is not ultimately blameworthy for killing Iphigenia, it nevertheless seems that it would be appropriate (and maybe even morally necessary) for him to feel remorse, frustration, guilt, and perhaps even disgust at his role in her death. After all, even if he is fully justified, it is nevertheless by *his own action* that a "father's hands are stained, [with] blood of a young girl streak[ing] the altar" (210–11). The real insight in Nussbaum's initial claim, then, does not depend on there being genuinely tragic dilemmas as she insists. Instead it is just that however he decides, Agamemnon will have to do business with the morally significant fallout of his choice, with the residue it leaves behind. Moreover, it's crucial to note that this residue—this value remainder—is not some abstract value that is left over. It's not, in other words, something that Agamemnon doesn't care about. Rather, what Agamemnon must do here necessarily entails destroying something—a person in this case—that he cares about deeply and truly identifies with. So the value remainder in question concerns Agamemnon's very own values and loves; that is, it concerns the deepest elements of Agamemnon's practical self.

We see something like this point in the text of *Agamemnon* itself, since regardless of whether the Achaean king acts wrongly and is so blameworthy or is simply "stained" by his decision, one thing is very clear: Aeschylus is highly critical of Agamemnon's action. In particular, he is especially critical of *how* Agamemnon makes and executes his decision to sacrifice Iphigenia. For despite an initial show to the contrary, Agamemnon does not seem to sufficiently struggle with or agonize over the tragedy of his choice in a way that is manifested in how he carries out Iphigenia's doom. And this last bit is key: it's not enough for him to be sad or to lament his choice—Agamemnon does this at the outset, after all. He also must recognize that the morally significant considerations that rationalize the sadness and lamentations in the first place are still action-guiding for him, even if they are outweighed by competing considerations (as they are in Agamemnon's case). That is, Agamemnon must understand that even if his love for his daughter should not (all things considered) move him to action, it nevertheless put significant constraints in *how* he is entitled to execute his decisions and *how* he should respond to himself in the wake of those decisions. Had he maintained his fierce love for Iphigenia, in other words, he might have still killed her, but he wouldn't just treat her as if she was nothing to him, as if she were no different from any other ritual sacrifice he needed to make at the start of war expedition.

To better understand the precise nature of Aeschylus's criticism and how he goes wrong, it's helpful to review the exact content of Agamemnon's deliberations and activity. Speaking of his predicament, Agamemnon says,

> Obey, obey, or a heavy doom will crush me!—
> Oh but doom *will* crush me
>   once I rend my child,
>     the glory of my house—
>   a father's hands are stained,
> blood of a young girl streaks the altar.
> Pain both ways and what is worse?
> Desert the fleets, fail the alliance?
>   No, but stop the winds with a virgin's blood,
>     feed their lust, their fury?—feed their fury!—
>   Law is law!—
>     Let all go well. (206–17)

Looking only at the first few lines of Agamemnon's speech, one can sense his awareness of the tragedy and also the rational necessity of his situation. But notice how quickly the tone shifts. He quickly moves from considering whether to feed the winds' lust and fury to an emphatic answer: "*feed their fury!*" And quite distressingly, we can almost hear Agamemnon rationalizing to himself the brutality that is to come: "Law is law!" These final statements suggest that Agamemnon, having briefly struggled with the impiety of filicide, is now ready carry out the required act. But surely a loving father, or indeed, *anyone* with a minimum of concern for other persons wouldn't turn so quickly from lamentations about one's situation to happily embracing the deadly "impurity" (218) of killing one's own daughter.

This quick shift portends Agamemnon's subsequent failure to fully appreciate Iphigenia's value and dignity. Aeschylus describes this failure when he tells us that just as Agamemnon makes his fateful decision, "his spirit [veers] black, impure, unholy," and "he stopped at nothing, / seized with the frenzy / blinding driving to outrage" (218–21). This outrage leads him not only to sacrifice Iphigenia but to sacrifice her as he would "a yearling" that must be gagged, lest her cries "curse the house" (234–36). Because he treats her as an animal, it is clear that having made the decision, Agamemnon fails to see how the reasons for refraining from sacrificing Iphigenia constrain how he kills her, and thus, he no longer recognizes her value in the way that a father should recognize the value of his child (and more generally, in the way that persons should recognize value in others).

It's clear, then, that for Aeschylus, the real problem with Agamemnon's behavior is not what he does but how he does it. In the face of tragic practical conflict, Agamemnon takes "the easy way out" and unequivocally resolves his will by simply dissociating himself from what had, until just a few moments prior, been a central aspect of his practical self. In other words, Aeschylus takes Agamemnon's initial ambivalence and distress to be short-lived and seems to regard him as subsequently making and executing his decision wholeheartedly.[7] For after the fateful decision is made, Agamemnon carries it out with a brutal and single-minded efficiency that would not be possible for a man who was still torn between his duties to his people and his duties to his child. Of course, even if he had maintained his ambivalence, given the rational necessity that he was faced with, we know that Agamemnon would have still carried out the deed. But in such a case, his actions and their meaning would have been fundamentally different. Rather than treating Iphigenia as an animal, he would have treated her as his daughter; he would have apologized for what he must do; begged her understanding and forgiveness; cried with her for her life, and for their shared torture; he would have left her ungagged, and cursed his house with her; his knife would have been guided not by the "frenzy" of a warlord but by the quickness of a father.

Bernard Williams has made a related point about backward-looking attitudes like remorse and agent-regret.[8] The idea that Williams stakes out is simply that if an agent is properly attuned to the values at stake, then in cases of practical conflict of the sort under consideration, a well-functioning agent will respond not with self-satisfaction or even a sense that she has done the unequivocally right thing. Rather, her response will involve some infusion of regret or remorse, since even in doing the right thing, her agency was implicated in causing serious harm.

Nussbaum echoes this point in her discussion of Agamemnon. As she puts it:

[7] Frankfurt has suggested that Agamemnon is forced to betray himself, since he is forced to choose between two motives that are "equally defining elements of his own nature." And while I agree that Agamemnon betrays himself at Aulis, it's not for the reason Frankfurt thinks. When Agamemnon "veers . . . unholy" with "outrage," it seems that what's so unholy and outrageous is that he finally and unequivocally stands behind his decision to sacrifice Iphigenia, not that he is ambivalent. For more, see Frankfurt 1999.

[8] See, e.g., Williams 1965, 1981.

The good agent will also feel and exhibit the feelings appropriate to a person of good character caught in such a situation. He will not regard the fact of decision as licensing feelings of self-congratulation, much less feelings of unqualified enthusiasm for the act chosen. . . . And after the action he will remember, regret, and, where possible make reparations. His emotion, moreover, will not be simply regret, which could be felt and expressed by an uninvolved spectator and does not imply that he himself has acted badly. It will be an emotion more like remorse, closely bound up with acknowledgement of the wrong that he has as an agent, however reluctantly, done. (Nussbaum 2001, 43)

Evidently, being a well-functioning agent is not simply a matter of selecting and bringing about some end. We must also be emotionally vulnerable to a wide range of retrospective responses—responses that reflect and express an awareness on our parts of the normative significance of our choices.

Williams's and Nussbaum's points are, I hope, relatively uncontroversial,[9] so to them I'd only add that a well-functioning agent will also take the very features of the conflict that retrospectively rationalize remorse and agent-regret into her initial deliberations in ways that, at the very least, affect how she makes and executes her decision. The after-the-fact failure of Agamemnon to feel the remorse that Nussbaum identifies for us is of a piece with his first, and to my mind, greatest failure: Agamemnon's failure to appropriately respond to Iphigenia's significance in his deliberations about what to do and how to do it. And, in the context of his practical conflict, this failure *just is* Agamemnon's failure to maintain ambivalence in the face of an unspeakably tragic dilemma, his failure to continue seeing his love for Iphigenia as having guiding authority. So just

---

[9] One might disagree with the details of Williams's and Nussbaum's analysis and yet still think the general point holds: one is not a good agent if one's emotional responses to choices that have suffering as part of their foreseen consequences are not muted in some way by remorse.

as an agent can be legitimately criticized for failing to experience regret after making decisions of a certain sort, so too, I contend, she can be legitimately criticized for failing to be ambivalent when making those decisions in the first place.

This point—that ambivalence is rationalized by the same considerations that rationalize retrospective emotional responses like regret and remorse—is suggested but not spelled out explicitly in the first bit of Nussbaum's description of how a well-functioning agent behaves in the face of tragic dilemmas. Recall, she claims that "the good agent . . . will not regard the fact of decision as licensing feelings of self-congratulation, much less feelings of unqualified enthusiasm for the act chosen" (2001, 43). These are, of course, responses you can have to a choice *after* you perform it. But they are also attitudes you can take toward possible actions you are considering during the process of deliberation. We can imagine, and indeed often do, the outcomes of various courses of action that seem open to us, and take as data how we anticipate ourselves responding to them. I might, for example, consider various options and conclude that I'll only be able to live with myself if I do that, or I will really regret it if I do this, or I will feel really good if I make that choice, etc., etc. These attitudes—which are really judgments about what I expect to feel in the wake of any given choice—at the very least often shape *how* I bring about my choice if not *what* I actually choose to do.

For that reason, I think that the attitudes that Nussbaum focuses on in particular here—feelings of self-congratulations or unqualified enthusiasm—can thus be key marks of not only an agent who retrospectively regards herself as having acted well but also of an agent who regards herself as being poised to act well. They can, in other words, be attitudes an agent takes about the proper structure of her will in the face of a practical conflict. But crucially, for Nussbaum, this is not how a well-functioning agent will regard her proposed choice in the face of a terrible dilemma like that of Agamemnon. A more equivocal "take" on the structure of one's will is what's called for in those circumstances. In other words, what she says here suggests an important connection between attitudes like regret and remorse on the one hand and ambivalence on the other.

Though Nussbaum does not do so, I think it's important to make this point explicit: the idea that good agents should not take their choices in tragic dilemmas to license self-congratulation or unqualified enthusiasm looks more or less like just another way of saying that a good agent would, were she to find herself in Agamemnon's shoes, maintain her ambivalence. "Self-congratulation" and "unqualified enthusiasm" are not literally the same as "self-love," "self-satisfaction," or "final and unequivocal" affirmation, of course, but they are attitudes one can take toward one's own will that are certainly in the same neighborhood as those that unificationists regard as necessary for well-functioning agency. It would be odd, then, if a good agent was to be self-satisfied but not self-congratulatory, and unequivocally affirming of her action but not unqualifiedly enthusiastic about it. It seems, then, that one way to interpret Nussbaum on this point is to see her as claiming that good agents, in addition to being disposed to emotions like regret or remorse in the wake of difficult practical conflict, will be ambivalent before their choices and maintain that ambivalence as they exercise their agency.

This point is important: if attitudes like regret are often a crucial sign of an admirably circumspect and responsive agent, we have good grounds for treating ambivalence in a more or less isomorphic way. Since there are good grounds for accepting the first part of this claim, then I conclude there are good grounds for accepting the latter. Agamemnon should have felt regret, as Nussbaum makes clear. But so too, I contend, he should have been ambivalent.

But this isn't all that goes wrong in Agamemnon's case. There is something even more terrible about his wholeheartedness. In particular, it seems that instead of saving him from self-defeat, Agamemnon's wholehearted choice and execution of that choice is precisely what *guaranteed* that his practical identity was destroyed. Before, he had valued being a warlord, king, brother, and father, but in his rush to maintain his commitment to the three former identities, he had to utterly demolish the latter. Practically speaking, Agamemnon was not the same agent in the wake of his choice. And the change wasn't too minor to remark upon, as might be the case when I decide to stop eating out so much, or listening to that podcast that only serves to rile me up, or staying away from an acquaintance who irks me. In those cases, my practical self changes slightly, but not in a way that can be described as self-betrayal. In Agamemnon's case however, the practical shift is so radical as to completely reorient him as an agent. It is the kind of change that might inspire a worried loved one to say, "I don't know you any more" and for that to be true.

By contrast, a response guided by ambivalence actually would have ensured that Agamemnon's will was properly responsive not just to what he has most reason to do in the moment of choice, but to who he is as an agent. In so doing, he would have been able to have genuinely maintained the part of who he was that loved his daughter. That is, in these circumstances, it is ambivalence and not wholeheartedness that would have preserved his integrity. In other words, it is ambivalence and not wholeheartedness that would have saved him from literally betraying an inner element of who he was. Accordingly, for Agamemnon, and for those in structurally similar conflicts, it is ambivalence and not wholeheartedness that is characteristic of well-functioning agency.

## 6.3.  Ambivalence and Integrity

Here we see that Agamemnon not only could have avoided an inherently self-defeating action by remaining ambivalent throughout his choice, but that it is precisely in becoming wholehearted in his commitment to the war effort that he is led to act in such a fundamentally self-defeating way. After all, Agamemnon's love for his daughter had previously been a significant aspect of who he was as an agent, so by dissociating himself from that love in the moments just prior to carrying out the sacrifice, and by coming to regard that love as not even putting some minimal constraints on how he might proceed, he makes himself into a new man—not literally a new man in terms of personal identity; instead a new man in terms of practical identity.[10] Since this is only possible because he gives up on a central aspect of his self, it seems that in circumstances like those that Agamemnon finds himself in, wholehearted endorsement of one motive or of one way of being as an agent is itself inherently self-defeating.

But this point holds for much more mundane dilemmas that we all face. If in the face of a deadline for accepting the new job offer, Erica fully dissociates from, say, her role as a caregiver for her parents—no longer seeing it as being in any way action-guiding—then she too would be guilty of a form of self-betrayal that is hard to live with. But if she maintains her ambivalence, then even if she decides to move on, we can expect that she will do so in a way that honors her love for her parents rather than "extrudes it as outlaw."

Now here you might worry that there is a key difference between Agamemnon's dilemma and Erica's: viz., that Agamemnon's dilemma is a conflict in identifying and Erica's is a conflict in willing. If so, Erica would count as having wholeheartedly resolved her ambivalence by ordering her priorities into a single determinate ranking. Nevertheless, wholeheartedness on her part will still be a form of self-betrayal. After all, if she is wholehearted in her decision to take the new job, and in so doing, decisive in prioritizing it over her concern for the care of her parents, then it seems that for Erica, any reason generated by her commitment to her career will outweigh reasons generated by less central elements of her practical self. But surely given her actual concerns, Erica should not be prepared to determine ex ante that she'll always prioritize work-given reasons over parents-given reasons. What's required for an

---

[10] For further development of this point, see Velleman 2002.

agent who cares deeply about her professional success and also for the welfare of her family is that she be flexible in weighing these values against one another. If Erica maintains her ambivalence, she is able to do this, since her will is fragmented in a way that leaves it indeterminate as to what she should do in future cases of conflict. Accordingly, she does a better job of preserving her integrity than she would if she resolved her conflict in willing by decisively and wholeheartedly ordering one volitional tendency over the other.[11]

Wholeheartedness, it seems, is often the source of, rather than the solution to, self-defeat and self-betrayal. But even though wholeheartedness does not guarantee integrity, perhaps it nevertheless serves as a basis for the kind of freedom that Frankfurt and other unificationists have long lauded. Indeed, in Agamemnon's case at least, it seems that his wholehearted endorsement of the war effort does in fact secure the kind of freedom that Frankfurt champions. After all, by dissociating himself from love for his daughter, it seems that Agamemnon enjoys "the inner harmony of an undivided will" and that "is tantamount to possessing a fundamental kind of freedom" (Frankfurt 2004, 97). This seems both correct and also deeply uninteresting. For though wholeheartedness frees Agamemnon from his internal strife, it's not at all clear that there is anything particularly attractive about this kind of freedom. Freedom from inner strife, conflict, or faction, as Plato, Frankfurt, and Korsgaard have all prized, seems good only *insofar as there is no reason to be engaged in inner strife, conflict, or faction*, and in Agamemnon's case, given what he values, there clearly are reasons to be so divided.

Of course, I should note here that one might think that the kind of freedom unificationists celebrate is ultimately attractive as a way of coping with the psychological distress of being torn. On this point, I actually agree; in fact I sympathize with Agamemnon much more than Aeschylus does, owing to the fact that I suspect he had

---

[11] Recall Razinsky's (2016) discussion of "compromise actions" for more on this point.

to make himself into a monstrous warlord in order to do what must be done. And this might very well have required that Agamemnon be wholehearted in his commitment to killing Iphigenia. Yet even if this is ultimately correct as an interpretation of what's going on in Agamemnon's case, it would only show that being wholehearted in the face of dilemmas can be instrumentally valuable. What it won't show, however, is that wholeheartedness is necessarily character-istic of well-functioning agency. So while Agamemnon's whole-heartedness is perhaps understandable as a human reaction to the horrible circumstances that he finds himself in through no fault of his own, it hardly seems to me to be the reaction of an agent whose will shows no defect.

Accordingly, the Argument from Self-Defeat fails. Being torn between multiple competing practical commitments is not analo-gous to having contradictory beliefs; nor does it necessarily ensure that an agent's activity is a self-defeating one. Nor does it mean that ambivalent agents lack integrity and an attractive form of freedom. In fact, as we saw with Agamemnon, only maintained ambiva-lence would have preserved his integrity, since only by maintaining his ambivalence would he have been able to do full justice to the competing elements of his antecedent practical identity without simply abandoning one of those elements.

## 6.4.  Conclusion

So far I have been engaged primarily in a negative project: to show that three powerful unificationist arguments—the Resolution Argument, the Affirmation Argument, and the Argument from Self-Defeat—all fail to show that ambivalence is necessarily a defect of the will. In what follows, however, I'll leave these unificationist arguments behind and focus more directly on explaining why I take ambivalence to be important, and why, in particular, I think that well-functioning agents must be open to ambivalence.

# PART II
# A WISE INCONSISTENCY

Do I contradict myself?
Very well then I contradict myself,
(I am large, I contain multitudes)
—Walt Whitman, "Song of Myself" (1855)

A foolish consistency is the hobgoblin of little minds,
adored by little statesmen and philosophers and divines.
With consistency a great soul has simply nothing to do.
—Ralph Waldo Emerson, "Self-Reliance" (1841)

# 7

# Normative Competence and Ambivalence

## 7.1. The Well-Functioning Agent

So far, we've considered how well unificationist arguments do in service of a conception of well-functioning agency. Not well, it seems. But a dearth of successful arguments for unificationism is not itself an argument on behalf of the conception of well-functioning agency that I want to defend. Accordingly, I turn now to the positive task of arguing that on no plausible account of well-functioning agency is ambivalence necessarily a problem. This claim might strike you as initially surprising, since we've considered theories of agency due to no less than Plato, Nietzsche, Harry Frankfurt, and Christine Korsgaard and at least identified those of many others—Augustine, Spinoza, Descartes, and Kierkegaard—that are apparently at odds with ambivalence. Nevertheless, there is a simple and powerful argument, at least in the way that any philosophical argument can be said to be "powerful," that well-functioning agency is not only compatible with ambivalence but might sometimes require it. The argument goes like this:

Argument from Normative Competence
(1) The well-functioning agent exercises her normative competence in all that she does.
(2) In some circumstances, exercising normative competence requires some degree of ambivalence on the part of the agent.

*In Praise of Ambivalence*. D. Justin Coates, Oxford University Press. © Oxford University Press 2023.
DOI: 10.1093/oso/9780197652398.003.0007

(3) So the well-functioning agent must be prepared to be ambivalent (in the event that she ever finds herself in circumstances of the sort referenced by (2)).

The simplicity of this argument notwithstanding, I think it is sound. All or almost all unificationists will accept (1)—though I'll say more about that below. (2) is obviously going to be the main source of controversy, so I plan on spending more time defending it. From these two premises, it follows that ambivalence is at least compatible with ideal agency, though, in the last part of this chapter, I will try to secure the slightly stronger conclusion: that the demands of well-functioning agency require us to be open to ambivalence, even if we are never in circumstances that warrant it.

## 7.2. How We Got Here

Before propounding the Argument from Normative Competence, I want to first recall that the property of normative competence has already played an important role in rebutting unificationist arguments. This, I hope, won't just remind us that normative competence might matter to discussions of well-functioning agency, but will also motivate the more pronounced role that this capacity plays in the remainder of the book.

In Chapter 3 I argued that an agent's ability to resolve the practical question that is before her (and so, her ability to resolve her will) does not require her to be wholehearted. The explanation for how an agent could be both ambivalent with respect to the dilemma she faces and also resolved in an authoritatively action-guiding way begins with the idea that as long as the agent's decision about what to do—i.e., her decision about what motive to license—issues from an exercise of her normative competence, then her will is resolved in an authoritative and action-guiding way. The reason for this is that in such a case, the agent choice reflects her "take" on what she has most reason do, all things considered.[1] In other words, she acts for what she takes to be good reasons. And surely decisions made on such ground have action-guiding authority.

The underlying premise behind this rejoinder to the unificationists' Resolution Argument is that when our decisions issue from an exercise of normative competence, then those decisions inherit the action-guiding authority of the reasons that the normatively competent agent is responding to. But, of course, you can be ambivalent and, without resolving your ambivalence, be moved to act because you, a normatively competent agent, saw that that one of the motives that was causing your ambivalence was responding to reasons that are weightier or more significant.[2] Voila! Resolving your will in an authoritative and action-guiding doesn't require that you be wholehearted, only that you be normatively competent.

In developing this response, I did not say too much about the exact nature of what normative competence ultimately consists in. A key reason was that, for this argument to work, it need only be the case that normative competence is compatible with ambivalence. This alone is an interesting result, but it isn't enough for an argument *for* thinking that well-functioning agents will possess a dispositional openness to ambivalence. After all, unificationists can agree that normative competence is compatible with ambivalence, while still holding that in cases in which normatively competent

---

[1] I say "take" here rather than "judgment" because I do not think that one's judgment about what one has, most things considered, reason to do is always authoritatively action-guiding (see Arpaly 2003). However, the agent's overall "take" on her normative circumstances and what matters in them might be a judgment on her part, though it might be an awareness that is located elsewhere in her moral psychology.

[2] In saying that the motive is "responding" to reasons rather than generating reasons, it's easy to read me as saying something that is at odds with Humean or other internalist theories of practical reasons. On that view, the motives in question generate (or are essential in explaining) why certain facts are reasons of the particular weight they are, but they are not (or at least need not be) responding to reasons that exist independently of the motive itself. I have much sympathy for this view, even if I am not ultimately convinced, so I want to be clear that what I say here is meant in a way that is consistent with Humeanism.

agents' actions issue from ambivalent wills, the agents in question are missing something crucial for "fully" ideal agency. What this means, then, is that to really see that unificationism is false, we'll need something stronger—viz., that normative competence actually can require agents to be ambivalent.

But why think this?

A key idea in the argument I developed in the previous chapter is that (at least) part of the reason Agamemnon fails as a well-functioning agent is that he doesn't act in a way that reflects any real understanding on his part of how the value of Iphigenia's life puts constraints on the way he can (legitimately) go about ending it. But this is just to say that although Agamemnon is himself a normatively competent agent in general,[3] he is not exercising this competence in his response to the circumstances in which he finds himself. This suggests that something like (2) was being presupposed by that argument, since precisely what alerts us to Agamemnon's failure to exercise normative competence in his circumstances is that he is wholehearted in his decision to execute his daughter and in his subsequent decisions as to how to carry it out.[4]

So I expect that if you've been with me so far—in particular, in my responses to the Resolution Argument and Frankfurt's version of the Argument from Self-Defeat, then you are probably already very sympathetic to the Argument from Normative Competence. However, you might instead be quite suspicious about what I've said so far in response to unificationist arguments against ambivalence. In that case, it's high time that I make my underlying normative assumptions explicit and offer arguments in defense of them—at least to the degree it is possible to make arguments in defense of underlying normative commitments. With this background in mind,

---

[3] If Agamemnon was not in general capable of exercising normative competence, then it wouldn't make sense for Aeschylus or his chorus to blame Agamemnon for his action.

[4] Of course, if I were less worried about begging the question against the unificationist, I'd just say here that something like (2) is *elicited* upon thinking about Agamemnon's case, and that the discussion of Chapter 6 serves as its own argument for (2).

I now turn to the task of more clearly elucidating what I take normative competence to be.

## 7.3. Normative Competence

On the view I favor, which takes as its starting point John Martin Fischer's (1994) account of guidance control, an agent is normatively competent just in case she possesses three connected, though conceptually distinct, capacities: sensitivity, attunement, and responsiveness. First, she must be *sensitive* to what reasons she has for action.[5] That is, she must have a capacity that enables her to recognize when some consideration is a reason for her to act in a particular way or to refrain from acting in a particular way. This is a requirement for normative competence because it is in virtue of this capacity that an agent is able to ascertain and understand which facts have the authority to guide her actions and which do not.

Of course, the requisite kind of understanding need not be judgmental in the traditional sense. An agent might possess this capacity in virtue of, say, her emotional sensitivity to others' needs. In such a case, she may not *believe* that she has reason to intervene on behalf of another's welfare at all. Perhaps she believes, if she has any beliefs about intervention at all, that she should not intervene. But even if this is true, insofar as she represents the normative fact in question via her empathetic and sympathetic concern, or in her indignation toward those who are causing the other to suffer, or in her deep sadness at the tragedy of another being made to suffer so,

---

[5] I formulate normative competence throughout as a rational capacity—i.e., a capacity that concerns reasons for action. However, I do this mainly for simplicity of exposition. You might think that it is both a rational and an evaluative capacity that concerns not only reasons for action but also values (this is my actual view), or even that it is simply an evaluative capacity. In the event you think that the normative domain is not exclusively rational but also evaluative, then it's possible to reformulate everything I say here in terms of evaluative competence without affecting the anti-unificationist argument I'm committed to defending.

then she is engaged in a form of moral cognition that is no less significant for rationalizing action than its doxastic counterpart.

Second, the normatively competent agent must be *attuned* to the normative weight of those reasons that she takes to bear on her practical situation, at least to a high degree of approximation. This element of normative competence is important because it's not enough, for example, that I correctly recognize the fact that my infant daughter is crying to be a reason to feed her; I must also be aware of or sensitive to the fact that it's a particularly weighty reason, one that is not outweighed by passing whims or flights of fancy.[6] If instead I am genuinely unable to recognize that these are *very weighty* reasons for me—if I am such that I really can't help but to think that the enjoyment I would experience by watching a rerun of something on television is more important than responding to her cries—then it's doubtful that I am a well-functioning agent. And the reason for this is simply that I appear to be an incompetent judge as to normative facts. Yet the incompetence isn't due to a complete unawareness of what facts matter but instead due to my lack of attunement to the degree to which those facts matter.

Finally, normative competence requires that an agent be *responsive* to her reasons, in accordance with their normative weight. In other words, be normatively competent, you must regularly act on the reasons you take yourself to have in a way that is commensurate with how weighty those reasons are in the circumstances you find yourself in. Of course, normative competence no more *guarantees* that an agent will act on her reasons in accordance with their weight than does competence at golf guarantee that the golfer will always

---

[6] This condition on normative competence is absent from many of the leading accounts of normative competence or, as it is sometimes called, reasons-responsiveness (see Fischer 1994, Wallace 1994, Fischer and Ravizza 1998, etc.). This omission is largely understandable, since it would be surprising if I possessed an ability to recognize that my daughter's cries were significant yet failed to correctly—at least to some high degree of approximation—identify *how* significant they are. Yet despite the surely close causal connection between being in possession of the former capacity and being in possession of the latter one as well, they are in fact distinct capacities, and it is crucial for normative competence that an agent has both.

start her putt on the exact line she should. Even very competent golfers sometimes pull or push their putts off line. Nevertheless, there needs to be a regular connection between one's sensitivity to reasons and attunement to their significance and how one subsequently behaves. In other words, the normatively competent agent needs to have robust dispositions to respond to their reasons in just the ways that those reasons rationalize.

As I understand her then, the normatively competent agent

(1) is sensitive to normatively significant facts, i.e., reasons;
(2) is attuned to the degree to which these facts bear on her practical situation, i.e., their normative weight; and
(3) is responsive to her reasons in accordance with their weight, i.e., is disposed to regularly act on the basis of her reasons in accordance with their weight.

Now obviously, each of these conditions invites a great deal of further clarification, but I think, for our purposes, we need not delve too deeply into the details of these conditions. One important reason for this is that I do not think it will ultimately matter for the Argument from Normative Competence whether one thinks, for example, that in order to satisfy (3) and be responsive to her reasons, the agent must, at the moment of choice, be able to act on or able to refrain from acting on those reasons, or whether it only requires a general capacity, such that given her recognition of some consideration as a reason, the agent acts on it in a nearby enough possible world.[7] Another reason is simply that what matters for the argument at hand is only the much more general and, to my mind, more important fact that normative competence, comprising these three capacities, provides us with a baseline for rational

---

[7] In other words, I want to set aside issues that arise in the context of debates about free and responsible *agency* and causal determinism. As I see it, even if incompatibilism about free will and moral responsibility is true, there might still be well-functioning (albeit not free or responsible) agents in deterministic universes.

agency as such. For the purposes of the Argument from Normative Competence, then, this ecumenical account of normative competence will suffice.

## 7.4. Normative Competence and Well-Functioning Agency

Recall that the first premise of the Argument from Normative Competence claims that well-functioning agents exercise normative competence in all that they do. In the preceding section, I offered an account of the *possession* of normative competence. As I said there, possessing normative competence does not guarantee that one will act in ways that reflect the one's underlying competence. But nor does it guarantee that the agent will always be sensitive to what reasons she has or attuned to how weighty those reasons are for her. Sensitivity, attunement, and responsiveness are modal properties, in that one's sensitivity, attunement, or measure of responsiveness is reflected not only in the nature of one's actual cognition, motivation, and action but in how one would think or feel about one's reasons or how one would act in other possible scenarios. But the exercise of a competence entails a kind of success—that that competence guided or otherwise causally directed one's *actual* engagement with the world.

Of course, even the exercise of competence does not guarantee success in what one is aiming at. On a gusty day, a competent golfer might start his putt on the right line, moving with the right speed to fall in the cup but still miss because the wind blew the ball fractionally off line. The fact that the golfer misses his putt certainly doesn't show that he isn't competent. Expert golfers, to say nothing of merely competent golfers, regularly miss many putts in a round. But this particular miss does not show that the golfer did not *exercise* his competence in his putt. He surely does, since there is real skill involved in recognizing the right line and the right speed and then rolling the ball on that line with that speed. The fact that he gets unlucky because of the wind seems irrelevant to assessments of competence (or exercises thereof) here.[8]

Because of factors outside of their control, it's true that the well-functioning golfer might shoot no better score than a maximally lucky novice. And yet only one of these golfers is someone an aspiring golfer should admire or try to emulate. The reason for this obvious: the well-functioning golfer's success is the result of regularly exercising a competence that he worked hard to develop. But the same holds for well-functioning agency. The truly well-functioning agent is one who isn't just in possession of normative competence. She's also someone who exercises or at least attempts to exercise her competence in everything that she does. In so doing, she is doing *all that she can* to bring about the object of her will. That is, she is doing all that she can qua agent. This won't mean that she'll always be successful or even that she'll be more successful acting in ways that reasons rationalize than a merely lucky counterpart. But it does mean that failure isn't attributable to a failure of agency on her part.

Naturally, you might think that there is more to well-functioning agency than simply being an agent who exercises normative competence in everything that you do. As we've seen, the unificationists clearly think this. But I'm not sure that this is right. What makes an ideal golfer, after all, is just that an agent is a competent golfer and that the degree of competence he has is maximized. There is no

---

[8] For what it's worth, there is real skill involved in even approximately reading a putt correctly and then responding well to that information. So a putt that is aimed on a fractionally incorrect line, perhaps one or two degrees to the left of the correct line, also might count as an exercise of the golfer's competence, since a novice would not even be able to get it in the ballpark of correct. This points to the fact that competence in a domain (and the exercise thereof) cannot require perfection in that domain—it must surely allow for some margin for error. So just as the exercise of golf competence will not, even excepting the role of circumstantial luck in determining the outcome of any particular shot, guarantee success, neither does the exercise of an agent's normative competence guarantee that she will be fully successful in recognizing, appreciating, and responding to reasons.

*further* requirement over and above that. You might say, well, the ideal golfer is as you've claimed, but also he always makes a hole in one on par threes and always holes out on his approach shots on par fours and par fives, "respects the game," never steps in his partner's lines, always cleans his divots and rakes his bunkers, dresses correctly, never talks during your backswing, etc. This might be. But really, I suspect that what you're really identifying here are not ideal-making qualities qua golfer. Instead, you seem to be merely listing aesthetic preferences you have about the kind of person you'd want to play with if you got to play with a truly well-functioning golfer.

Similar reasoning applies in the case of well-functioning agency. You might worry, for example, that a normatively competent agent who is perfect with respect to her sensitivity to reasons, attunement to their weight, and responsiveness to those reasons in accordance with their weight is not yet ideally well-functioning qua agent. For that, you might insist, she must be wholehearted, or unified, or have a fully integrated will, or be able to unequivocally affirm all of her choices, or love herself, or be self-satisfied. But here again, these things all seem less like the basis for the agent's being better qua agent. We might naturally prefer agents who possess these qualities, or when imagining ourselves at our absolute best, think we'd prefer to be wholehearted, self-satisfied, able to unequivocally affirm our choices, etc. Notice however, that these things, if they happen for anyone, *even idealized agents*, take a lot of good luck, in precisely the same way getting a hole in one on every par three would take unimaginably good luck even for the maximally well-functioning golfer. For this reason, I'm tempted to think that it's possible to spell out well-functioning agency exclusively in terms of normative competence. But whether you are in agreement with this claim or not, the Argument from Normative Competence does not depend on normative competence being a sufficient basis for well-functioning agency. It only requires something much weaker: that a well-functioning agent will, whenever she acts, do so in a way that exercises her normative competence. And this, I think, is very hard to deny.

## 7.5. Exercising Normative Competence in the Face of Practical Dilemmas

As I said at the outset of this chapter, I fully expect that premise (2) of the Argument from Normative Competence to be where most of the philosophical action is. To remind you, that premise states:

> (2) In some circumstances, exercising normative competence requires some degree of ambivalence on the part of the agent.

If this premise is true, then ambivalence can be a manifestation of an agent's normative competence *rather* than an impediment to it. But why think that this is true?

The short answer is that sensitivity, attunement, and responsiveness to reasons require agents to structure their wills in ways that reflect the relative worthiness of a range of competing courses of action. But to fully see how this works, it will be helpful to return to Aulis, since explaining what goes wrong with Agamemnon when he decides to wholeheartedly embrace the execution of Iphigenia can be traced to a failure on his part to fully exercise his normative competence.

Aeschylus details the Chorus's critical response to Agamemnon as follows:

> And once he slipped his neck in the strap of Fate,
> his spirit veering black, impure, unholy,
> once he turned he stopped at nothing,
>> seized with the frenzy
>>> blinding driving to outrage—

wretched frenzy, cause of all our grief!
Yes, he had the heart
   to sacrifice his daughter,
  to bless the war that avenged a woman's loss,
    a bridal rite that sped the men-of-war.

"My father, father!"—she might pray to the winds;
no innocence moves her judges mad for war
Her father called his henchmen on,
  on with a prayer,
    "Hoist her over the altar
like a yearling, give it all your strength!
She's fainting—lift her,
   sweep her robes around her,
  but slip this strap in her gentle curving lips . . .
    here, gag her hard, a sound will curse the house"—

and the bridle chokes her voice . . . her saffron robes
pouring over the sand
     her glance like arrows showering
wounding every murderer through with pity
   clear as a picture, live,
she strains to call their names . . . (217–41)

There is a lot here, but a key point seems to be that once Agamemnon "slip[s] his neck in the strap of Fate" (217), we are told that his attitude toward his daughter changes in an indefensibly *radical* way. It is as if once the decision was made, he no longer took her intrinsic significance or his love for her seriously, even though just prior to the decision, the thought of killing her causes him great anguish.

This gets us to the real problem with how Agamemnon makes and executes his choice, a problem that I introduced in Chapter 6 but want to explore more completely here. For Agamemnon, we can see that the very same considerations that made his anguish a rational response to the situation *initially* are still present as he chooses and carries out his choice. These considerations, which include the facts that his daughter is valuable, that he loves her dearly, and that her welfare is central to his own conception of a life worth living, might not, all things considered, justify sparing her in this tragic context (following Nussbaum, I'm imagining that they do not). Surely, however, they are not thereby *silenced*—i.e., they still have some practical import.[9] This means that the reasons there are to refrain from sacrificing Iphigenia retain an important role in determining precisely *how* Agamemnon should go about executing his decision. Unfortunately, Agamemnon ignores this secondary role that the reasons to spare his daughter's life might play in rationalizing his subsequent behavior. And this, as I suggested in Chapter 6, is precisely how he fails.

The Chorus describes this failure by telling us that at the moment that Agamemnon makes his fateful decision, "his spirit [veers] black, impure, unholy," and "he stopped at nothing, / seized with the frenzy / blinding driving to outrage" (218–21). This outrage leads him to not only sacrifice Iphigenia, but to sacrifice her as he would "a yearling" that must be gagged, lest her cries "curse the house" (234–36). His outrage also makes it impossible for Agamemnon to have the appropriate attitudinal response to what he has been forced to do. He treats Iphigenia as an animal, and so it is clear that having made the decision, Agamemnon fails to appreciate that the reasons for refraining from sacrificing Iphigenia, though outweighed, still *constrain* how he kills her. In other words,

---

[9] John McDowell (1979) introduces the idea of silencing in the context of distinguishing virtue from mere continence. The virtuous individual won't count present danger as a reason to run away that is simply outweighed. Rather, "The risk to life and limb is not seen as any reason for removing himself" (335). It's possible that McDowell is right about this in the case of virtues, though later in this chapter we'll see some reason to doubt this. Yet even if he is, it is dubious that if Agamemnon had been virtuous (assuming virtue requires him to sacrifice Iphigenia) then he would have regarded the cost of her life as being no reason at all.

the real problem with Agamemnon's behavior—how he fails—is not *what* he does but *how* he brings it about.

By contrast, if Agamemnon had exercised his normative competence—if he had continue to appreciate that reasons for refraining from killing Iphigenia had, if not action-determining authority, a kind of action-guiding or, better, action-*constraining* authority even though they were outweighed—then he would not have carried out the execution the way that he does. The reason for this is that part of what's required to be a normatively competent agent is that the agent sees, is attuned to, and is responsive to the value and normative significance of *countervolitional* reasons—i.e., reasons for acting in ways that are contrary to how the agent does in fact act.

## 7.6. Countervolitional Reasons

Countervolitional reasons are ubiquitous, as is our general appreciation of their normative significance. Despite this, they figure less in contemporary thinking about how agents' wills should be structured than they ought. To see this, let's consider the case of Siobhán.

Siobhán has a tough decision to make. She loves her partner, but she also knows things with him aren't going so well. It has recently become clear to her that the things he wants in their relationship going forward are actually quite different from the things that she wants. And though their personalities are a good match, their goals and ambitions have changed a great deal over their years together. They still make each other happy, but also increasingly frustrated. So after months and months of uncertainty and concern, it now seems clear to Siobhán that she has to decide whether to stay in the relationship and make some real changes to her priorities or to end the relationship. Of course, the fact that there are good things and bad things about either choice makes her want to just ignore the problem, in the hopes that things will improve. But ultimately (and wisely) Siobhán reasons that being passive in the situation would be worst of all. *She's* going to make the choice, she tells herself, rather than just let things happen to her.

Part of what makes Siobhán's decision so difficult here is that given her values, there are powerful reasons for choosing either course of action. That you love someone is itself a weighty reason for trying to make things work, even if means refiguring some of your other priorities. Not everyone gets to have what Siobhán has had with her partner, and for those who have had such experiences and valued them, it will seem important to preserve the relationship. Of course, it's important to be honest with yourself: no matter how valuable a relationship might be, if things just aren't going to work, they're just not going to work. Moreover, Siobhán worries that if she stays with her partner, then she'll have to ultimately betray many of her deepest goals and ambitions. Perhaps there might be some circumstances in which we should compromise these things, but Siobhán's reasonably sure that she shouldn't give up on so many of her aims so easily. Maybe if her partner were going to do something unfathomably cool, like become an astronaut, she'd be willing to go wherever he needed to be. Or maybe if he were to devoting himself to something incredibly admirable like opening up a clinic in a historically underserved community . . . But as things actually stands, she thinks that the goods of self-actualization give her weighty reasons to resist settling for her partner's modest and slightly selfish priorities.

Other considerations feature in Siobhán's deliberations as well. These are perhaps less normatively significant than those I have already mentioned, but they're no less human, and they're certainly recognizable as such. Among other things, Siobhán worries about how her friends and family will react. For example, she can already hear her great-aunt chiding her that "she's not getting any younger" upon hearing that she has broken up with her partner. By contrast, she can also imagine future conversations with her parents, who would be disappointed that Siobhán sacrificed her promise for her partner's successes. Of course, she knows that maybe there's not too much to these thoughts, particularly to those she imagines coming from her great-aunt, but she also can't shake them. Like most of us, Siobhán does not want to be lonely. But she also doesn't want to feel stifled and minimized.

As Siobhán and, I expect, the rest of us already know, figuring out what to do in situations like this can be quite trying. To figure out what to do, we ask ourselves (more or less explicitly) about the considerations for and against the possibilities we're confronted with. We also want to know which of our values we'll be forced to compromise in selecting either option. And in most cases, even many cases in which such things cannot be determined, we want to know what the expected value of either choice comes to.[10]

Of course, even if we can ascertain all of the relevant considerations (no small feat!), we'll still need some metric that will allow us to "weigh" or "balance" apparently incommensurable values against one another. Unfortunately, however, knowing how to balance competing considerations in any particular context is extremely difficult. Moreover, even if you're lucky and you manage to get a grip on how to weigh things in the particular set of circumstances you currently find yourself in, you might quickly discover that that's no help in formulating the balancing measure in a way that will generalize to putatively similar circumstances. Indeed, it often seems that when faced with a difficult practical conflict, we rely on a balancing measure that helps us get by in that situation but leaves us out to sea the next time we're confronted with a seemingly impossible choice. That is, when faced with significant decisions, many (perhaps most) agents tend to rely on a balancing measure that is, if not inarticulate (as Aristotle claims), certainly inarticulable for *the agent*. An oddity of this experience is that here,

---

[10] However, perhaps, as L. A. Paul (2014) has argued, it is simply not possible to know how good an alternative would be if, in order to pursue that option, you would have to transform yourself.

in the situation in which we are most *active* as a person, we are nevertheless opaque to ourselves.

But look, once we're clued into the relevant considerations and balancing metric—whatever that metric is and however we arrived at it—we (tend to more or less) decide what to do in such cases by the messy process of weighing up what's to be gained (and lost) by opting for one course of action and then comparing those gains (and losses) to the gains (and losses) that are reasonably associated with the other course of action. Then, assuming we aren't akratic, we'll decide to act on the deliverances of this process. We will, in other words, *exercise* our normative competence. And then we live happily ever after. Or something like that.

In any case, making difficult decisions of the sort that Siobhán is faced with is just half the battle. For suppose that after careful deliberation, Siobhán reasonably decides to break off her relationship. Having made this decision, Siobhán must now execute it. This follows from her decision, of course. But what's less clear, and what we tend to give less thought to, is the question not of what to do but of how to do it. In Siobhán's case, it seems that all things being equal, she has reason to end the relationship in a way that she wouldn't have if the nature of the relationship had been different. She shouldn't, for example, just ignore her partner until he takes the hint.[11] Nor should she just text him or send him a one- or two-sentence email. However this isn't because it's categorically wrong to break up with someone in these ways. It's just that in cases like Siobhán's, the specifics of her relationship affect what she owes to her soon-to-be-former partner.

One important difference between what Siobhán has reason to do and what a couple that's only been together for a short time has

---

[11] The "should" here is not meant to be moral, though there are of course moral considerations that bear on the entrance and exit conditions of our interpersonal relationships. So if Siobhán fails to act as she should here, she's legitimately subject to not a moral judgment, but something more like the judgment that she's been a bad friend.

reason to do is that Siobhán has weighty but, as she sees them, insufficient reasons to refrain from breaking off the relationship. Accordingly, in Siobhán's case (but not in the case of folks who have only been out together a few times), given that she has decided to end the relationship, these reasons will consequently become considerations that should factor into her subsequent deliberations concerning *how* she should break up with her partner in a way that takes seriously what he's meant to her during their time together. And plausibly, something that would be especially callous in the circumstances, like sending a text to end the relationship, fails to do this. In other words, the means that Siobhán can take to break off the relationship are constrained in ways that they wouldn't be if she had only been seeing her partner for a short time. And the explanation for this is simply that although the reasons she has for staying with her partner might ultimately be outweighed, they aren't thereby *silenced*. As a result, they continue to have practical import in constraining the range of ways in which Siobhán can legitimately execute the decision she takes herself to have most reason to perform. So, because Siobhán still loves her partner, since she still thinks he's basically a stand-up guy—just someone who no longer shares with her the same ambitions—she should break up with him in a way that basically respects these facts.[12]

The moral of Siobhán's story, which I hope is fairly intuitive, is simply this: Siobhán's *countervolitional reasons*—which are reasons to perform some action that, in the course of deliberation, an agent has decided to not act on—can still have a significant normative role to play in structuring Siobhán's subsequent attitudes and behavior. And an agent cannot ignore this secondary role that rational considerations play in constraining our behavior if she is genuinely exercising her normative competence.

---

[12] The story works in reverse as well. If Siobhán decides that she should stay with her partner, then it seems the fact that she needs more support will constrain the terms on which she'll allow the continued relationship to proceed.

The lessons for Agamemnon (and from the rest of us as well) are clear. His love for Iphigenia and her value as a person are very weighty reasons for him to refrain from killing her. They're so weighty that in just about every conceivable set of circumstances it would be morally disastrous for Agamemnon to act contrary to these considerations. Perhaps the horrifying circumstances that Agamemnon finds himself in are the lone exception. But while he might have, all things considered, reasons to execute his daughter, the weightiness of his reasons for not killing her cannot simply be ignored. To do so would be to fail to be fully sensitive to what reasons he has and attuned to their weight. Which is just to say that to do so would necessarily involve a failure to exercise his normative competence. And because an exercise of normative competence in this set of circumstances will lead Agamemnon to sacrifice Iphigenia in a maximally humane and respectful way, it will mean that he is still recognizing his love for her as being *authoritative* for him, as a motive with which he continues to identify. In other words, the fact that this motive retains its authority to constrain Agamemnon's actions means that he has not extruded it as outlaw—he has not dissociated himself from it or its reasons-giving force. But this is just to say that he is not wholehearted. That is, if he maintained his commitment to loving Iphigenia as being the source of weighty reasons for him, Agamemnon would have been ambivalent. Thus, to act in a way that exercises his normative competence—which is necessary for well-functioning agency—Agamemnon must proceed with a fragmented will.

This vindicates the key premise in the Argument from Normative Competence, which holds that in some circumstances agents exercise their normative competence only if they are ambivalent. As a result, the argument itself is sound: well-functioning agency sometimes requires that agents be ambivalent. By itself, this is on the one hand a significant result: unificationism must be false. However, you might worry that this result is, practically speaking, relatively unimportant—perhaps very few of our practical conflicts are like

Agamemnon's in that there are weighty enough countervolitional reasons so as to rationalize ambivalence on the agent's part. If such conflicts are few and far between, then something near enough to unificationism might turn out to be true. On the other hand, if such cases regularly arise in the course of our lives, then we'll have grounds for thinking that insofar as we are normatively competent, we'll be disposed to regularly be ambivalent.

As it happens, I think that this latter possibility is in fact the case: circumstances in which exercising normative competence requires some degree of ambivalence on the part of the agent are ordinary. They arise primarily (but not exclusively) in three sorts of conflicts: first, conflicts exclusively within the moral domain; second, conflicts that arise in the domain of and between moral and nonmoral values; and, third, in conflicts between projects or commitments that agents regard as meaningful for their lives. Since all three of these types of conflicts occur frequently, human agency at its best cannot be conceived of as being at odds with ambivalence. But this argument, the Regularity Argument, will have to wait until Chapter 8. Before we get to it, I need to first consider a possible objection to the practical significance of countervolitional reasons.

## 7.7. Skepticism about (Some) Countervolitional Reasons

Although it *seems* quite clear that countervolitional reasons are often present and relevant for determining how we should act, not everyone is so sanguine that there are reasons of this sort or that, if there are, they are nearly so weighty or ubiquitous as I'm making them out to be. Perhaps the clearest argument against them, at least when it comes to conflicts between the demands of deontic morality and nonmoral ends, comes from Christine M. Korsgaard (2009), though as we'll see, her argument (if sound) will have consequences for other sorts of conflicts as well.

In developing an account of the proper structure of deliberation, Korsgaard argues that considerations which in some context might constitute reasons for action are, when found to be in conflict with morality, *no reason at all* for the agent. That is, they are completely silenced and so, for a well-functioning agent, irrelevant for correct practical reasoning. This model of how we should think about what to do stands in stark contrast to the one I've been presupposing. On my preferred model, what we do when we're thinking about what to do is weigh competing reasons against one another and act in whichever way the balance of reasons recommends. This applies not only in cases of nonmoral conflicts, but also in the case of conflicts between our moral and nonmoral commitments.

The problem with this model of deliberation, Korsgaard tells us, is that it presupposes that reasons have some normative significance independently of how a well-functioning agent would use them in her deliberative activity. That is, it seems there is a kind of substantive realist commitment to thinking that our reasons have weights that are not themselves a function of the norms of practical reasoning. But Korsgaard (1996) rejects substantive realism on the grounds that it cannot supply an explanation for why moral facts are normative for agents who do not care about being good. On Korsgaard's alternative, then, we cannot deliberate and then settle our wills by first considering how weighty the reasons for and against a particular course of action are and then proceeding to act on the basis of what we have most reason to do in a way that is constrained by sufficiently weighty countervolitional reasons because there are no such independent facts about what we have reason to do. And in particular, she explicitly rejects the reasons-giving force of considerations of the sort I've been treating as the basis of weighty countervolitional reasons.

As she puts frames her alternative:

> On this view, the way you are supposed to deliberate is to for-
> mulate a maxim, stating the complete package of considerations

that together favor the performance of a certain action. . . . Your maxim, once formulated, embodies your proposed reason. You then test it by the categorical imperative, that is you ask whether you can will it to be a universal law, in order to see whether it really is a reason. Universalizability is a condition on the form of a reason, and *if a consideration doesn't meet this condition, then it is not merely outweighed—rather, it is not a reason at all.* (Korsgaard 2009, 51; emphasis added)

The key bit here, at least for our purposes, is that for Korsgaard, *no* consideration that does not emerge unscathed from a process of correct practical reasoning is a reason at all. This means that Korsgaard is generally skeptical of there ever being any reason to act immorally.

What Korsgaard's view means for us is that in many cases in which ambivalence appears to be warranted, there would no countervolitional reasons, and so ambivalence in those cases would in fact be irrational. The reason for this is simple. Suppose that an agent is torn between participating in a protest for a just cause that is liable to turn violent and staying comfortable and safe at home. And suppose that as she is deliberating about what to do, this agent comes to believe that any maxim that involves violence fails the test that determines the condition on the form of a reason. Then, on Korsgaard's view, there is no reason whatsoever for her to go. And supposing that a maxim of staying home when you otherwise would be prone to engage in violence passes the relevant test, then it follows not only that the agent should stay home but that she has no reason not to stay home. But if she has no reason not to stay home, how could it be rational for her to be ambivalent about what to do? After all, ambivalence comes with a feeling on the part of the ambivalent agent that her choice will necessarily leave some value remainder in its wake. In this case, however, that wouldn't be true on Korsgaard's view, since there would be nothing of valuable left on the table by the choice to stay home. The agent's feelings to the contrary are therefore inapt and ill-fitting, and so she should not have them. Thus, if Korsgaard is correct, ambivalence won't be justified.

For those who are not attracted to unificationism, this already seems to be a good reason for rejecting Korsgaard's alternative account of deliberation and practical reasons. This argument won't do much for reasons externalists either, since they are happy to reject Korsgaard's suspicion of substantive realism.[13] But there is another reason—one that is neutral with respect to the thorny debates about reasons internalism vs. reasons externalism and substantive realism vs. constructivist antirealism—for thinking that Korsgaard is wrong here. As Mark Schroeder (2007) has forcefully argued, we are very bad judges as to the conditions when judgments about negative reasons existentials—judgments of the form, "there is no reason to $a$"—are true. In particular, we regularly assert there to be no reason for $a$-ing in cases in which there clearly are. And unfortunately, Korsgaard's model of practical reasoning gets things wrong in precisely the way Schroeder's error theory predicts, not only in mundane sorts of conflicts agents might experience but in Agamemnon's case as well.

To see this, consider what Korsgaard's model would predict about an agent who has an opportunity to go see his favorite baseball team play (imagine that the team is visiting from out of town) in a big playoff game but who has promised to help a friend move during the same time the game is occurring. On the Kantian view Korsgaard develops here, the fact that the agent would have a lot of fun at the game is *no reason at all* for her to go to the game given that she has promised her friend to help her move. And this is true even though, absent having made the promise, *the very same fact* (i.e., that it would be a lot of fun for the agent) would have been a weighty reason for her to go to the game. But this implication is odd. Of course, I agree (or am at least tempted to agree) that in

---

[13] For examples of substantive realists, see Scanlon 1998 and Parfit 2011.

general agents shouldn't break promises just to have fun. This is simply because I, like many others, think that moral reasons are typically quite weighty, perhaps even decisively weighty in contexts such as this. Thus far at least, Korsgaard and I are not in necessarily disagreement about what the agent should *do*.

The problem with Korsgaard's account, however, is that it affords no weight to the fact that by going to the game, the agent would have a great deal of fun. To see why this is a problem, consider someone else who promised a friend that he would help her move. But suppose this person doesn't like baseball at all, finding baseball games to be interminably boring. Now suppose that both of these agents break their promises in order to go to the game. According to the view Korsgaard presents, because neither agent had any reason at all to go, both of their actions are equally objectionable, immoral, and irrational. However, this is puzzling, since although both agents act in ways that are (by hypothesis) not ultimately defensible, the former agent's action is not only explicable but also, it seems, partially justificatory. She won't be able to fully justify herself to her friend on the grounds that the game was awesome, of course. But her friend might at least *understand* why she broke her promise. Moreover, the bereaved friend will probably appreciate that there was *something* in favor of going to game, even if she's not happy about it.

This point becomes clearer when we're thinking about whether the fun of going to the game matters retrospectively. For although I could forgive a friend who broke a promise so that she could have a uniquely fun experience, I would find it very difficult to forgive someone who broke a promise to me in order to do something she hates—what must that say about her attitudes toward me, after all? These differential responses suggest that even on the assumption that each act of promise breaking was wrong, one of them had something going for it that the other did not. In other words, it suggests that even considerations that do not in themselves license action can be reasons. What explains all this, I think, must simply be that the baseball-loving promise breaker, and not the baseball-hating promise breaker, acted for a reason. True, she *shouldn't* have acted for that reason. But that doesn't mean it was no reason at all, as Korsgaard claims.

We can say the same thing in Agamemnon's case. Suppose Korsgaard is right that there is a single source of reasons, and suppose for the sake of argument that Nussbaum is right to think that only by killing Iphigenia can Agamemnon be fully rational. If that's right—and here I want to set aside whether this is the verdict we'd get if we asked a moral absolutist like Kant or Anscombe (1958) or Korsgaard herself about Agamemnon's dilemma[14]—then on the model of practical reasoning Korsgaard is proposing, Agamemnon will have no reason at all to refrain from killing his daughter. Accordingly, the fact that he loves Iphigenia should play no role in his deliberation about what do or in how he brings about the state of affairs that reason commands. But if he deliberates and acts in a way that reflects this putative fact, then it looks like he cannot be a good agent in the way Nussbaum describes, since there is no reason to feel bad about what you've done if there was no reason to have refrained from doing it in the first place. Yet this is precisely what Korsgaard's view commits us to. Agamemnon, on this view, should be wholehearted in his decision to sacrifice Iphigenia because ambivalence would betray an allegiance on his part to some motive that has zero rational support.

I think it's this implication of Korsgaard's skepticism about countervolitional reasons that makes her account ultimately untenable. There are often weighty reasons to do otherwise that, even if they do not suffice to rationalize a specific course of action, do

---

[14] It is fine to set this issue aside because if we suppose the absolutist view that would not allow the sacrifice of an innocent for *anything*, then we can run the argument backward. Even if it's true that an agent should never kill an innocent person, we wouldn't be indifferent between an agent who kills innocents for the fun of it and one who does so because he's trying to save his civilization. This suggests that even on the strong absolutist assumption that it's always wrong to kill innocents, there might be circumstances in which there is at least some reason to do so.

provide the agent with guiderails or constraints on how to proceed. The wholehearted agent dispenses with such guiderails, since he regards motives pulling him to the contrary as being having no action-guiding authority for him. On the other hand, the ambivalent agent is sensitive to these reasons in both deliberation and action. When she acts, then, hers is a genuine exercise of normative competence.

## 7.8.  Conclusion

As I've said, I do not think a plausible normative theory can deny the existence of weighty countervolitional reasons in conflicts of the sort that Agamemnon faces. Consequently, were a well-functioning agent in Agamemnon's shoes, she'd have reason to *maintain* rather than excise her ambivalence. Unificationism is therefore false.

But again, you might accept this and still think that this is all very inconsequential. It perhaps suffices to show that unificationism is false, but it does not show that something near enough to unificationism to merit its name is false. After all, if conflicts of the sort Agamemnon faces are exceeding rare, then it might be extremely likely that for any actual agent, she will never be in a circumstance that merits ambivalence on her part. The disposition to be open to such ambivalence would only need to be a very weak one— hardly worth considering when thinking about how one should be as an agent who faces the kinds of choices and conflicts that actual agents typically face. I take up this challenge in Chapter 8. There I will argue that the circumstances in which agents can be rational for being ambivalent are *regular*.

# 8

# Morality and Meaningfulness

## 8.1. The Regularity Argument

Because we are normatively competent agents, because we are sensitive to, attuned to, and responsive to reasons and values as the authoritative guides of our actions, we should be open to being ambivalent. But how strong must this disposition be? It might be very weak indeed if we very rarely or perhaps never find ourselves in situations in which there is a conflict between things we value or care about that cannot be resolved without value remainder of some kind. In fact, if we could be reasonably sure that such a conflict would never or almost never occur, then openness to ambivalence wouldn't seem important at all. This sort of certainty seems possible, however, only in exceptional, perhaps inconceivable circumstances. Perhaps if the Christian conception of the afterlife is true, then we will someday live together without tears or strife in the presence of God. There we'll have unlimited opportunities to pursue any and all of the activities that seem worthwhile. Without scarcity of time or emotional and material resources and without ignorance of the good, which plague us in this life, perhaps it's doubtful that we'd ever have to worry about running into a situation in which there was *necessary* inner conflict of the sort that Erica faces. In such a world, there might be little reason for ambivalence.[1]

Alas, this is not the world we currently find ourselves in. Our world is one in which there are many conflicts between things that

---

[1] It might be, then, that Augustine's suspicions about ambivalence stem from his wanting to bring a little bit of heaven to earth.

*In Praise of Ambivalence*. D. Justin Coates, Oxford University Press. © Oxford University Press 2023. DOI: 10.1093/oso/9780197652398.003.0008

we care about, value, or otherwise regard as important. It is one in which we must make our choices knowing full well that we are finite and limited in our power, knowledge, and time, such that by making *this* decision rather than *that* one, we are meaningfully cutting ourselves off from an attractive or worthwhile alternative. Unlike the saints in heaven, we *have* to choose between *inter alia* ambitions and attachment, between moral commitment and love. In fact, if we humans, who are limited in all the familiar ways, value or love or care about *anything at all*, then I suspect this fate will be hard if not impossible to escape no matter what it is in particular that we love. Accordingly, it is my suspicion that a well-functioning agent, one who regularly exercises her normative competence, will not only be disposed to feel ambivalent but will frequently find herself actually divided over the practical dilemmas she faces.

The work of the Regularity Argument is to transform this suspicion into a well-founded conclusion. As we'll see, the explanation why the domains of morality and meaning respectively create ambivalence-meriting conflicts is straightforward. In each of these broad domains there is either a plurality of goods that can be realized *or* a single good that can be realized in a plurality of ways.[2] But in either case, whether the agent finds herself conflicted about distinct goods or about distinct-yet-incompatible ways of realizing the same good, she'll therefore have grounds for ambivalence.

Of course, this bare statement of the key premises of the Regularity Argument is not itself sufficient. We need to carefully consider these twin domains of human concern in order to see how they are structured such that our involvement in that domain will regularly present us with ambivalent-meriting conflicts. I'll start

[2] I frame things disjunctively here because I want to be ecumenical with respect to normative ethical theories and theories of meaningfulness. So if you're a pluralist, as I am, then the explanation we'll see for the regularity of ambivalence-meriting conflicts will be grounded in distinct goods. If you reject pluralism, then the explanation is not grounded in distinct goods but in the frequency with which *the* good can be realized in independent and distinct ways.

with the domain of morality, a realm of oughts and shoulds and pro tanto reasons and virtues, and then explore the domain of meaning. What we'll find, however, is that the explanation for why the moral domain is and should be generative of ambivalence on the part of well-functioning agents is more or less parallel to the explanation for why caring about living a meaningful life will also induce ambivalence in well-functioning agents. Consequently, whether you care about one or both of these domains, if you are normatively competent, you should regularly expect to be faced with ambivalence-meriting practical conflicts.

## 8.2.  Morality

Theories of morality concern what we are required to do, what we should or ought to do, or what we have weightiest reasons to do given that we live our lives with other rational agents who have disparate interests and concerns. Moral theories also concern what patterns of behavioral and attitudinal dispositions we should cultivate given our natures as rational and social creatures. But whereas theories of morality agree (more or less) about their subject matter, there is a great deal of disagreement as to the source (or sources) of those moral facts. This disagreement is familiar from foundational debates in normative ethics. Kantians, for example, think that the source of deontic morality is the law that the rational will gives itself—viz., the categorical imperative.[3] Utilitarians, by contrast, think that the source of morality is uniquely found in the intrinsic goodness of pleasurable states.[4] Beginning in the twentieth century, it has been increasingly common (though by no means uncontroversial) for moral theorists to defend some kind of value pluralism.[5] On this family of views, there are a number of intrinsic

---

[3] Kant 1998; Herman 1993; Korsgaard 1996; Engstrom 2009.
[4] Bentham 1907; Mill 1998; Sidgwick 1874; Smart 1973.
[5] Moore 1903; Ross 1930; Nagel 1979; Railton 1984; Chang 2015.

goods—love, respect, friendship, fidelity, achievement, giving people what they deserve, happiness, knowledge, solidarity, and pleasure, to name a few—that independently serve as the basis for morality. Along with this trend, there has also been a resurgence of ethical theories that locate the source of moral facts in the virtues.[6] These views tend to have a perfectionist element, identifying specific dispositions as virtues because of the necessary connection between those dispositions and an excellent or well-lived human life.

There is, of course, a great deal of controversy as to which, if any, of these views most accurately describes morality. Luckily, we can ignore much of this controversy since, as it happens, each of these views yields the same result: no matter whether you're a Kantian or a utilitarian or a pluralist or a virtue theorist, it will follow that if you're concerned about morality, you shouldn't be surprised to find yourself facing ambivalence-meriting conflicts. The Regularity Argument will therefore succeed given the truth of any of the major normative ethical theories.

## 8.2.1. Pluralism

Since it is perhaps easiest to see how the truth of some form of value pluralism would support my contention that we regularly find ourselves in circumstances that merit ambivalence, I want to begin here. After all, if moral reasons are ultimately grounded in distinct and independent values, there is no reason to think that those values will only apply when their promotion does not conflict with the promotion of any other value.[7] And indeed we often see many of the goods, values, or choiceworthy ends that pluralists identify as being sources of moral conflict. For example, the value of friendship

---

[6] Anscombe 1958; Watson 1990; Foot 2001; Lear 2005.

[7] I speak here of "promotion," but it is not at all obvious that what all values call for is promotion. Some call for appreciation or admiration, others respect, and still others honor.

supplies me with a weighty reason for giving a struggling friend a job. Yet the value of giving people what they deserve supplies me with a weighty reason to give it to a more qualified candidate. In such a case, if I care about my friend's plight, I'll probably feel pulled to help her (and in so doing, reciprocate many of the good things she has done for me over the years). And yet, if I also care about fairness and giving people a chance when they've really earned it, I will feel strongly motivated to hire the well-qualified candidate.

Of course, this doesn't mean that it's morally permissible to act on each of these motives. It's quite plausible, after all, that I'd act wrongly by giving the job to a friend over a clearly more qualified candidate. But this doesn't mean that my desire to hire a friend is an immoral motive as such. It's clearly not, as fidelity to friends and benefactors, generosity, and beneficence are genuinely moral values. Nor does the fact that they are clearly outweighed in this particular situation mean that ambivalence is necessarily misplaced. Indeed, how could I be a good, conscientious friend if I wasn't at least somewhat divided in the face of this practical conflict?[8]

An even more general form of moral conflict is one that arises when there are powerful reasons for paternalistic intervention. In such cases, we are forced to weigh the value of beneficence against the value of personal autonomy. For authoritarian types, this sort of conflict isn't particularly worrying, owing to the fact that individuals with such dispositions do not care much about the value of giving others a great deal of freedom to direct their own lives. But for those of us who do value this, while also valuing providing aid for those people (or at least, preventing them from harm), there is a real tension here. For example, those of us who teach students who aspire to go on to graduate school in philosophy (or any other

---

[8] It is sometimes said that a friend is someone who helps you move and a good friend is someone who helps you move the body. As a norm of friendship, this almost certainly goes too far. However, what I say here suggests a more plausible alternative: a good friend is someone who will at least some ambivalence when offered the chance to help you move the body.

academic discipline) often feel this tension quite keenly, and as a result are often quite ambivalent about the degree to which we should encourage them. Yet ambivalence in the face of their requests for advice is not a deficiency on our parts. It is instead a manifestation of our normative competence—our sensitivity to the powerful reasons for *both* encouragement and caution. And conflicts like this are hardly unique to undergraduate advisers. They are the stuff of parenting, policy decision-making, medical care, pedagogy, and more.

Practical conflicts of these sorts feel much more familiar than Agamemnon's. But if pluralism is true, then their familiarity isn't some surprising, hard-to-explain thing. It simply owes to the fact that (given pluralism) the moral realm is fragmented in an important way. And because there are many different values that are relevant to morality, if we care about being moral—something that almost all of us do care about—then we'll have grounds for caring about goods that come into conflict. And this will inevitably result in inner faction, at least insofar as we are sensitive to and attuned to the significance of the goods in question. Yet this is precisely what well-functioning agency requires. So if pluralism is true about moral values, then a normatively competent agent's concern for being moral will regularly make it the case that there are grounds for her to be ambivalent.

## 8.2.2. Kantian Monism

If the Regularity Argument required pluralism to be true, then it would (at least in my estimation) still be sound. But it would not be convincing to *monists* about morality, who hold that there is only one source of value that is relevant for deontic morality. However, this is precisely what many unificationists think; indeed we've already seen this with Korsgaard's (2009) insistence that there are never reasons to act in a way contrary to the deliverances of the categorical imperative. This means that if the best that I can do is successfully argue that a well-functioning agent must be open to ambivalence *given* a conception of value and morality that unificationists antecedently reject, I haven't done all that much.

I think, however, that appeals to monism as a defense of unificationism are ultimately misguided. As we'll see, given the actual *content* of leading forms of monism, we should expect agents to face ambivalence-meriting practical conflicts with more or less the same regularity we would expect given pluralism. The reason for this is quite easy to see in the case of Kantian monism. According to this view, deontic morality has its source in the normative standard that rational agents give themselves. This is the categorical imperative, which tells us that we should "act only in accordance with that maxim through which you can at the same time will that it become a universal law" (Kant 1998, 4:421).[9] And while this principle is often thought to put rigid constraints on what can and what cannot be a moral basis for acting, it's considerably more open-ended than that. Accordingly, even if this principle is the sole source of all of moral reasons, the resultant moral landscape will nevertheless serve as fertile grounds for ambivalence-meriting practical conflicts.

We see this clearly in the case of duties of beneficence. According to Kant, we owe succor to those in need. But this duty does not have specific realization conditions, in the same way that many other duties do. For example, the duty that I have to not attack you without provocation can be met only if I do not attack you without provocation. By contrast, the duty that I have to help a hungry person can be discharged in a variety of ways. I can give the person money so that he is able to buy food. I could also buy food for him

---

[9] Kant himself provides multiple formulations of this principle that he insists are equivalent. I have my doubts, though for the purposes of this discussion, I'll take him at his word. If, however, Kant is wrong, then his view is also a form of pluralism, which locates the source of moral considerations alternately in a purely procedural good (i.e., universalizability), human dignity (i.e., treating all persons as ends in themselves), and the goods of a harmonious social order (i.e., relating to others as if in a kingdom of ends).

directly. Or I could hire him at a fair wage that does not exploit his current situation and so provide him a continuous stream of resources. To fulfill my duty, it's not particularly important which of these options I choose, only that I choose one of them. It's here, in cases like this, that what *I care* about matters. This is just to say that duties of beneficence are what Kant called "imperfect duties," i.e., duties about which idiosyncratic inclination can affect the methods by which agents can reasonably go about satisfying their duties.[10]

Now if there were only one person to whom duties of beneficence were owed, then ambivalence about which way to satisfy one's duty of beneficence would be silly. Just decide how you're going to help the person and move on. But alas, there are always a great many people who are in desperate need of our help. Our resources, financial and otherwise, are not typically up to the task. Given the limitations of most of our bank accounts as well as our psychological capacities, we have to make very difficult decisions about which needy individuals we're going to support. Am I going to bail out this protestor who was wrongfully imprisoned for exercising her right to assemble and seek redress from her government, or am I going to donate to a fund that pays for prescriptions for individuals who do not have healthcare? If I *care* about each of these causes and the people who are helped by then, then, according to the categorical imperative, I will have powerful reasons to support each of these causes. But at the margin—either at the margin of what I'm obligated to do in support of others, or at the margin of what I'm capable of doing financially—I have to make a choice. And given what I care about, and given the fact that however I choose, there will be some value residue in having made *that* choice rather than the alternative, it seems that the duty of beneficence serves as a source for ambivalence-meriting conflicts.

---

[10] I agree with Thomas Hill (1971) in thinking that the way that Kant formulates the distinction between perfect and imperfect duties is a bit more complicated than is suggested by what I say here. For our purposes, however, those complications should not affect the argument of this section, so I happily omit them here.

An isomorphic argument can be made even more forcefully in the case of the Kantian duty to develop one's talents. About this duty Kant says, "As a rational being, a person] necessarily wills that all the capacities in him be developed, since they serve him and are given him for all sorts of possible purposes" (1998, 4:423). It is, of course, impossible to fully develop all of one's capacities. We have limitations of time, psychological power, and access to useful form of instruction that interfere with the full development of our capacities. So as a result, we'll have tough decisions to make about which capacities we develop. (Kant might say "your rational capacity, of course" but this imagines that our rationality is grounded in a single faculty, "Reason," which, of course, is quite dubious.)

Here again, we have an imperfect moral duty. As a result, inclination plays some role in shaping how we proceed in developing ourselves. One might want very much to live "the life of the mind," but the skills needed to do this well are not the only skills that we have reason to develop. Developing one's sense of empathy or sympathetic concern is also a meaningful capacity to work on. So too, developing social virtues seems important. But the capacities that are at play in these skills are not the same as the ones that are involved in developing one's intellect. And if a person cares about each of these domains, as one should, then if that person is normatively competent, we should expect her to feel some ambivalence in deciding how to prioritize her own self-development.

The existence of conflict in these cases very clearly does not require that there are independent source of moral obligations. The mere fact that I am required to help others or to help myself is enough. And the reason for this is simple. Even if only one thing matters—say, acting in a way that can be willed as a universal law—if there are multiple ways of realizing that one thing, there will be room for meaningful forms of ambivalence. So if the agents who must resolve moral conflicts have disparate concerns or values that pull them toward realizing what morality requires in mutually incompatible ways, then they will have grounds to be ambivalent. But this is precisely the situation we regularly find ourselves in. And so the moral domain will prove to be a fertile source of ambivalence-meriting conflicts even if the Kantians are correct to think that universalizability is the only thing that matters morally speaking.

### 8.2.3. Virtue Ethics

The tradition of virtue ethics locates the source of morality in the set of behavioral and attitudinal dispositions that must be possessed in order to live an excellent human life. Some versions of virtue ethics seem to be simply forms of pluralism, in that the relevant dispositions contribute to human excellence because they render the agent prone to do and think and feel things that are good for their own sake. On this view, the fact that virtues are connected to an excellent human life is due to the prior normative significance of the values that each of the virtues secures. More commonly, however, virtue theorists tend to insist on the explanatory primacy of character (e.g., Watson 1990). On this view, what morality requires of us is that we act in a way that is governed by and consistent with what virtue requires. And since virtues are character traits that are themselves *constitutive* of human excellence, it follows that morality requires of us that we act in a way that facilitates our own excellence.

On the pluralist interpretation of virtue ethics, one can expect to find ambivalence-meriting conflicts with no less frequency than would be the case given any other version of value pluralism. The reason for this is simply that on this view, the behavioral and attitudinal dispositions in question are virtues *because* the kinds of activities and attitudes they secure and promote are independently good. But for pluralists of this stripe, many distinct things are independently good. And nothing about their value guarantees that they will not come into conflict with other things of value. So in the event that they do conflict, as, for example, is often true in the case of conflicts between the values of justice and mercifulness, we will, insofar as we are virtuous (or weaker: care about being virtuous) and normatively competent, find ourselves ambivalent.

In the case of the more perfectionist account of virtue ethics, the argument that being virtuous (or being sufficiently concerned with virtue—one can face difficult practical conflicts even if one has not fully attained sagacity) frequently leads to ambivalence-meriting conflicts looks different. The reason for this is that on this view, a character trait counts as a virtue because of its necessary role in facilitating and constituting human excellence. You might therefore be tempted to think virtues cannot come into conflict in ambivalence-meriting ways. After all, an excellent human—at least according to virtue theorists in the Greek tradition—is one who will have the knowledge to discern, for example, just how much justice or just how much mercy is called for. And so she will apparently have no grounds for being ambivalent about responding to wrongdoing with mercy instead of justice (or vice versa), since surely she will be disposed to dole out the correct amount of each. More generally, one might think, since all the virtues jointly facilitate human excellence, it seems likely that they must be unified in some deep way.

Nevertheless, I think it is a mistake to think that perfectionist strands of virtue ethics will prove problematic for the Regularity Argument for two reasons. First, I think that much of what Kant says about imperfect duties to oneself—particularly the duty to develop one's talents and capacities—is perfectionist in nature (see Hurka 1993). And as we saw in our discussion of that duty, the substantive question of how to go about developing oneself in these ways generates a variety of ambivalence-meriting conflicts. It seems to me that this would be no less true for an agent aspiring toward virtue. The fact that a virtuous agent will have the practical knowledge necessary to discern how to adjudicate between justice and mercy does not mean that she does not feel the force of both justice and mercy independently. Nor does it mean that she does not experience her inability to choose, say, mercy in a particular circumstance as unfortunate. Indeed, the mere fact that she's cultivated robust dispositions to be both just and also merciful suggests that those dispositions will be activated when appropriate and also that the agent will approve of each outcome at least to some degree even if, because of her virtue, she would not act on one or another of these motives in some specific set of circumstances.

This point follows from the fact that acts of virtue require agents to exercise their normative competence. After all, the virtuous agent will recognize that her initial approval of both justice and mercy constitute reasons for exercising both justice and mercy. So even if one of these is not all-things-considered choiceworthy in the circumstances she finds herself in, that option (i.e., the one that the virtuous agent does not choose) will nevertheless provide her with countervolitional reasons, at least in ordinary circumstances. (This seems particularly true in the case at hand, since one cannot have reasons for mercy without there being reasons for justice.) As a result, it follows that the presence of weighty reasons to do otherwise will affect the structure of the virtuous agent's will even if they do not determine which option she pursues.

The second reason I suspect that a virtuous individual will regularly find herself in ambivalence-meriting situations comes from substantive judgments about how the virtuous agent will respond in especially difficult practical dilemmas. Or to put the point slightly differently: there is a virtue required for human excellence that disposes the virtuous agent to regularly be ambivalent. We already saw the initial basis for such a claim in Chapter 6. There, I argued that Martha Nussbaum (2001) was correct to think that virtuous agents would have felt remorse and regret had they faced the choice that Agamemnon did. How else to explain Agamemnon's failure in that situation? But Agamemnon's dilemma, which reveals the degree to which human pursuits are subject to capricious external forces, is structurally isomorphic to a great many moral conflicts that we all regularly experience. So virtue for us, at least insofar as we, like Agamemnon, are also subject to the vicissitudes of life, also seems to require a disposition to feel remorse and regret for our actions in the face of hard moral conflicts.

Susan Wolf (2001) has offered a more perspicuous treatment of this disposition—this "nameless virtue"—which she takes to be activated in cases of moral luck.[11] Concerning this virtue, Wolf writes:

> There is a virtue that I suspect we all dimly recognize and commend that may be expressed as the virtue of taking responsibility for one's actions and their consequences. It is, regrettably, a virtue with no name, and I am at a loss to suggest a name that would be helpful. It involves living with an expectation and a willingness to be held accountable for what one does, understanding the scope of "what one does," particularly when costs are involved, in an expansive rather than a narrow way. It is the virtue that would lead one to offer to pay for the vase that one broke even if one's fault in the incident was uncertain; the virtue that would lead one to apologize, rather than get defensive, if one unwittingly offended someone or hurt him. Perhaps this virtue is a piece or an aspect of a larger one which involves taking responsibility not just for one's actions and their consequences, but for a larger range of circumstances that fall broadly within one's reach. (2001, 13)[12]

[11] Wolf focuses on cases like those discussed in Williams 1981, but the point applies to tragic dilemmas of the sort that Nussbaum discusses. For that reason, I take it that they are discussing the same virtue.

[12] It's my view that Wolf's nameless virtue is a species of magnanimity. The magnanimous individual is one who has a great soul, where this is understood (*pace* Aristotle, *Nicomachean Ethics* IV.3) as both a willingness on her part to take on for herself more burdens than she deserves to bear and also a willingness to lighten the burdens that those around her bear. (So understood, Hester Prynne from Nathaniel Hawthorne's *The Scarlet Letter* [2007], Mrs. "Marmee" March in Louisa May Alcott's *Little Women* [2007], Rev. John Ames in Marilynne Robinson's *Gilead* [2004], and Lou Maytree in Annie Dillard's *The Maytrees* [2007] all exemplify this virtue.) As I see it, the nameless virtue is therefore a form of magnanimity because in the case of an agent who takes responsibility for the consequences of her action when they were due to luck, she is strictly speaking taking on more than she is required to by desert. In so doing, she is also lightening the burdens of those on whom the consequences of what she's done will naturally fall.

Here Wolf puts some conceptual meat on the bones of Nussbaum's proposal. After all, because remorse and regret are attitudes that one experiences in virtue of having taken responsibility for the baleful consequences of an action even if that action wasn't wrong for the agent, it's plausible that this is precisely the virtue that Nussbaum herself identifies as being lacking in Agamemnon.

If Nussbaum and Wolf have in fact identified a real virtue—and I think they have[13]—then as a substantive matter, the virtuous individual will be disposed to take responsibility and therefore feel remorse and regret for what she has done even when it's not her fault that she was in the circumstances that led to that action. But as I already argued, just as fitting remorse and fitting regret are retrospective markers of normative competence, by reflecting the agent's sensitivity to countervolitional reasons, ambivalence similarly manifests an exercise of normative competence. Thus, if dispositions to take responsibility contribute to human excellence in a way that is constitutive of virtue, then, so too, dispositions to be ambivalent when significant values are at stake should also contribute to human excellence. In other words, just as we're rightly suspicious of those who are never disposed to feel remorse or regret,[14] we'd do well to be suspicious of the wholly wholehearted.

Of course, this alone won't show that this nameless virtue will regularly be activated in the well-functioning agent. Yet here it's worth considering just how frequently we are faced with moral choices between genuine moral values—between justice and mercy or between friendship and fairness or between equanimity and moral indignation, to mention but three such conflicts. This is no less true for the virtuous agent, since she too is sensitive, attuned, and responsive to these considerations. Yet in how many of these cases are we "dimly" aware that regret or remorse are often fitting

---

[13] The fact that we are prone to admire those who are disposed to have this virtue attests to this.

[14] "No Regrets" is a famously bad tattoo, but it's an even worse principle to live by.

responses to our dilemmas, in light of the goods that are left on the table after the fact? A great many it seems. But this just means that our sensitivity, attunement, and responsiveness to these things should manifest itself and guide our wills with no less frequency. In other words, it just means that if virtue theory is true, then insofar as we care about developing virtuous dispositions, we'll often recognize ourselves as facing ambivalence-meriting conflicts.

## 8.2.4. Utilitarianism

Utilitarians are value monists who hold that the only thing that matters for its own sake is pleasure (i.e., they are hedonists). To this, they add a commitment to maximizing pleasure. Utilitarian moral theorists therefore conclude that our moral obligations are all grounded in the principle that we act in whatever way will create the most pleasure possible.[15]

Now at first glance, utilitarianism seems the moral theory that is least likely to require ambivalence of normatively competent agents. After all, according to utilitarianism, any practical conflict that you face is between bringing about states of affairs whose value can be reduced to the amount of pleasure contained therein. So if I see that giving money to this charity that I care about will cause $X$ amount of pleasure and that giving money to another charity that I care about will cause $2X$ amount of pleasure, then if I am normatively competent, I will always choose the second charity over the first. Yet in such a case ambivalence doesn't seem called for. By analogy, if I offer you the choice of $1,000 no questions asked or

---

[15] This too is an oversimplification that obscures numerous controversies that occur between self-identified utilitarians. But again, I plan on simply ignoring these controversies (as I did in the previous section) since the aim of this section is simply to show that even if one accepts a form of value monism, moral conflicts can regularly arise that merit ambivalence on the part of normatively competent agents. This point, however, only requires that we assume something that utilitarians of all stripes accept: that hedonism is true.

$500 no questions asked, it would be awfully strange if you felt ambivalent about taking the former offer. Because there is a direct one-to-one comparison you can make between what's gained and lost by taking either option (i.e., because the goods in question are fungible), it seems that there's just no room for ambivalence once one understands what the best option is.

This is certainly correct as far as it goes. But I'm doubtful that it goes very far. For starters, it leaves open the possibility that the value of two options might create the same amount of pleasure. So this means that if each charity uses the money equally effectively to produce pleasure, then I might reasonably find myself feeling ambivalent about which option to choose. Of course, I imagine that such cases are extremely rare, so even if this point holds, it won't suffice to show that given utilitarianism, we should regularly expect to find ourselves in moral conflicts that merit ambivalence.

A deeper problem with utilitarianism is that the varieties of pleasures we can experience seem less given to meaningful one-to-one comparisons than utilitarians typically care to admit. J. S. Mill, of course, recognized something along these lines when he distinguished between "higher" and "lower" pleasures. But the real issue here doesn't rely on his distinction. Instead, it is simply that there are important qualitative differences between kinds of pleasure that make it not only hard to directly compare pleasures but also doubtful that all pleasures are fungible.[16] The pleasure you experience when you qualify for the Boston Marathon seems different in kind from the kind of pleasure you experience when you hungrily take a first bite into a perfectly cooked steak. And this pleasure is in turn quite different from the kind of pleasure you experience when you decline to order steak on moral grounds. Pleasures that come from hard-won achievements, sensuous experiences, and moral scrupulousness (or maybe just smugness if your motives are less pure) are all pleasures, but they are not obviously fungible in the way

---

[16] This "disunity" objection can be traced to Henry Sidgwick (1874).

hedonism often suggests. And it seems reasonable that individuals could care about each of these different types of pleasures. Now this does not mean that utilitarianism or hedonism is false, but it does suggest that even committed hedonists can, by their own lights, find themselves in situations that merit ambivalence, owing to the fact that you might have good reason to care about qualitatively distinct types of pleasure that resist direct one-to-one comparisons.

Naturally, many hedonists will object to this.[17] What feels like a qualitative difference, they contend, is really just an inability on our parts to discern the exact hedonic comparisons. Still, even if this hedonist response is correct, it won't show that hedonists are never required to be ambivalent. To see this, we need only to consider the so-called paradox of hedonism, which alleges that in the long run, more pleasure is created if pleasure is not aimed at as an end in itself. A common illustration of this point comes from friendship. Friendships can be extremely pleasurable relationships. As a result, a maximally pleasurable life (for humans at least) will almost surely involve some close friendships. But if you want to have a close friendship, you should not make choices within the friendship that are aimed at the creating the most pleasure. Rather, you should act in ways that treat the friendship as valuable for its own sake, since in so doing, you'll better promote and sustain the friendship itself.

On just this point, Peter Railton (1984) has powerfully argued that a *sophisticated hedonist* will be one who recognizes this fact and values some ends (like friendship) for their own sake instead of just seeing them as mere conductors for pleasure. This requires inter alia that when one is deliberating about what to do, one does not always go back and try to reduce the value of the end in question to the amount of pleasure it will create because this is precisely the overly instrumentalist orientation that prevents us from getting the most pleasure possible. But once you've done this—that is, once you've come to care about and value a variety of activities for their

---

[17] See, especially, Broad 1930.

own sake and regularly treat them as such in practical reasoning—
then at least in principle you will find yourself in moral conflicts
that merit ambivalence on your part.

Railton takes this point even farther, arguing that recognition of
these facts should push one away from *believing* hedonism at all.
This won't mean that hedonism isn't true, but it seems that for the
same reason that a sophisticated hedonist is likely to have more
pleasure than an unsophisticated one, someone who believes pluralism to be true is likely to have more pleasure than a sophisticated
hedonist. After all, even if we hold fixed that hedonism correctly
identifies the objective criterion for determining what one ought to
do, it seems plausible that one will get much more pleasure by living
in a way that refuses to instrumentalize not only goods like friendship but also respect, solidarity, love, generosity, beauty, giving
people what they've earned, and so on. But if this is correct—if the
best way to be a hedonist is to live as if hedonism is false (and, insofar as this is possible, to *believe* that hedonism is false)—then the
hedonist will have reason to live as a pluralist. But as we already
saw, that involves valuing a wide variety ends of precisely the sort
we saw to come into conflict with one another earlier. In other
words, it involves regularly finding oneself in situations that merit
ambivalence.

## 8.2.5. Moral Conflict and Ambivalence

We've now seen that at least four very different accounts of the relationship between moral standards and value each require us to be
ambivalent, at least insofar as we care about morality and are normatively competent. That is, if you care about your moral duties,
then you will often find yourself confronted with situations in
which you must prioritize one motive with which you identify at
the expense of another and, in so doing, be moved to act in a way
that leaves something of value on the table. And just as this kind of

situation licenses (and indeed, might *require*) regret or remorse of some form retrospectively, so too it warrants ambivalence.

Of course, not everyone cares about morality directly. And if a certain kind of reasons internalism is true, then in principle, we do not necessarily have reason to care about morality. On such a view, which has found many able defenders, an agent is not irrational in virtue of giving *no* weight to moral considerations.[18] In other words, if an agent neither cares about morality nor cares about something else that supplies her with (at least) instrumental reason to be moral, then she is within her (rational) rights to simply ignore the "demands" of morality. We might complain that she's bad and insist that we do not want to be around such a person, but that doesn't mean that she's a defective *agent*. The grip of morality might therefore be quite tenuous on the structure of our will. And if so, then it's hard to see how the fact that moral conflicts can merit ambivalence hurts unificationism as such. It might be, if this sort of Humean internalism is true, that well-functioning agents in the relevant sort of conflict should simply prefer to revisit their level of concern (if any) for morality instead of being ambivalent. Maybe, in other words, Agamemnon and not the Chorus had the right idea in Aulis.

But even if this view provides us with a conceptual possibility of being rational but in no way caring about moral ends or morality *de re*, it is not ultimately an attractive one. Avoiding ambivalence-meriting conflicts by ignoring something that's genuinely important or by not caring about morality at all, such that its standards have no rational say in how I should conduct my life, means giving up too much. Morality does not create ambivalence-meriting conflicts because it is at odds with integrity as a matter of course. Far from it. Morality is the source of ambivalence-meriting conflicts precisely because it values our integrity—recall, it is sometimes possible to

---

[18] This view is traditionally attributed to David Hume (2000), but Bernard Williams (1979) and Harry Frankfurt (2004), among others, have more recently endorsed it.

preserve your integrity only if you are ambivalent. That is, morality is the often the source of ambivalence-meriting conflicts because it respects the fact that *we* all matter even though social conditions that facilitate this fact must balance a multitude of competing interests and concerns.[19]

## 8.3.  Meaning

Yet morality is just one practical domain that is the source of difficult, ambivalence-meriting conflicts. The practical domain that concerns what we must do in order to live meaningful lives is similarly suffused with such conflicts. As a result, our lives, at least if we want them to be meaningful, are likely to be filled with choices that demand at least some measure of ambivalence. The reason for this is that the conditions for a meaningful life almost always require agents to be personally invested in a variety of goods. But caring about, valuing, or being deeply invested in a variety of goods leaves one open to all sorts of deep, personal conflicts. By sheer dumb luck (or perhaps Providence), one might value lots of distinct goods and yet never experience the sort of conflict that is necessary for ambivalence. But this bare possibility offers no guidance to agents who are not so lucky. The rest of us, upon whom Providence has not shone so warmly, must determine how to live given the existence of such conflicts.[20] Accordingly, I argue, a meaningful life requires

[19] It is chic to imagine morality to be an inconvenient burden, or worse, a form of enslavement (e.g., Williams 1985), but in fact, morality plays an important role in securing a kind of freedom—one that facilitates the pursuits of a diverse set of individual ideals. This point has its source in Saint Paul, Leibniz, and Kant, among others, but has found more recent expression in Strawson 1961.

[20] Now, again, the agent facing such a conflict *could* cut volitional ties with one of the sources of ambivalence. But this "solution" does little to solve the problem at hand, since typically at least, our lives don't become *more* meaningful by cutting ties with some subset of the important things we might care about or value. Alternatively, she could radically deprioritize something she cares about. But this seems inauthentic at best, and a form of self-betrayal at worst. It's better, I therefore conclude, to be ambivalent.

regular willingness on the part of the well-functioning agent to be ambivalent. Consequently, ambivalence isn't just a fitting response to existentially significant conflicts of a sort that rarely arise; the circumstances in which it is apt are ubiquitous.

To develop this premise of the *Regularity Argument*—that being concerned to live a meaningful life will supply an agent with regular opportunities for ambivalence—I will first explore how meaningfulness as such is at odds with single-minded devotion to any particular good or activity. A meaningful life, we'll see, typically involves having reasons to care about many distinct goods and activities. But in turn, this diverse pattern of concern leaves us regularly vulnerable to conflicts that are impossible to resolve without value remainder. As a result, therefore, to live a meaningful life, an agent must be prepared to experience ambivalence with some frequency. Between this and the arguments of the previous section, which show that caring about morality will also require well-functioning agents to be open to ambivalence, I conclude that the Regularity Argument has a solid grounding.

## 8.3.1. Two Theories of Meaning

To develop this argument in more detail, I will consider two recent accounts of meaningfulness—Susan Wolf's (2010, 2015) *Fitting Fulfillment View* and Thaddeus Metz's (2013) *Fundamentality Theory*—but I hope what I say here will generalize to other plausible theories of meaningfulness as well. I begin, then, with Wolf's theory of meaning.

According to Susan Wolf's Fitting Fulfillment View,

A life is meaningful insofar as its subjective attractions are to things or goals that are objectively worthwhile. That is, one's life is meaningful insofar as one finds oneself loving things worthy of love and able to do something positive about it. *A life is*

> *meaningful, as I also put it, insofar as it is actively and lovingly*
> *engaged in projects of worth.* (Wolf 2010, 34–35; emphasis added)

What this view identifies with a meaningful life is a life in which an agent is deeply invested in and engaged with various things that have genuine value. So for example, the life of a two-bit huckster, whose life has been largely devoted to making money by exploiting sick, elderly, and otherwise vulnerable people (think here of Manley Pointer, the door-to-door Bible salesman from Flannery O'Connor's [1971] "Good Country People"), doesn't seem to be a particularly meaningful one. The reason for this, Wolf would counsel, is that the things that this shady character seems to care about and the goals he has attempted to pursue are not very valuable. On the other hand, authors like Marilynne Robinson or Alice Munro, who have produced some of the best literature written in the English language over the past forty years, and who clearly care deeply about their work, seem to be living more meaningful lives. And the reason for this is that what these authors value and have committed their lives to has significant value.

Thaddeus Metz's Fundamentality Theory of meaning shares some features with Wolf's, but has a more rationalist flair. According to Metz, "A person's life is more meaningful, the more that she employs her reason and in ways that positively orient rationality towards fundamental conditions of human existence" (2013, 222).[21] What this means is that your life is meaningful to the degree you use your rational capacities—which for Metz include all "judgment-sensitive attitudes" (i.e., attitudes that are responsive to judgments an agent makes about what reasons she has [see Scanlon 1998])—in ways that leave you positively oriented toward the most basic or fundamental conditions on our lives. This set of

---

[21] Metz goes on to clarify this definition of meaning in a variety of helpful ways, but for the purposes of this argument, the further amendments are not relevant. Since they invite a number of complications, I omit them from this discussion.

conditions includes the goods that are required (in a basic or fundamental way) for our individual and collective lives and the environment in which we live our lives.

Metz relies on the case of Nelson Mandela, whose life is a paradigm of meaning, to illustrate these points. In particular, he claims that this is because Mandela's life work was oriented toward promoting social structures and policies that promoted equality and welfare and toward ending activities that undermined tyrannical and oppressive policies. As he puts it:

> Freeing people from discrimination and tyranny and providing them with urgent medical assistance are forms of positively orienting one's rationality towards conditions of a characteristic human being's life that are responsible for much else about her life, of two sorts. First, they are positive responses towards others' rational nature. Rational nature, particularly as it is manifested in autonomous decision-making, is largely responsible for much about the course of a normal human's life. Promoting equality and liberty, and improving others' health, are substantial, constructive responses to people's reflecting and their choosing consequent to it. . . . Now, another respect in which at least Mandela's life was meaningful . . . concerns the way his rational nature was positively directed towards shared conditions of life. (Metz 2013, 227–28)

These fundamental conditions on individual and shared human life—the conditions of equality, welfare, autonomy, etc.—are the basis for meaning in the way that alternative ends that people might merely *want* or *enjoy* do not. Thus, Metz's account also rules out the meaningfulness of a huckster's life; swindling people is not a fundamental condition of shared human existence, after all. So too, it rules out trivial ends, even if they're ones we all (or almost all) share. It's for this reason that Mandela's actual life was meaningful but a counterpart Mandela who succeeded only in ensuring that the people of South Africa had well-kept toenails would not be. We all like well-kept toenails, of course, but they are in no way fundamental to our individual lives or our collective existence.

Now, as I see it, both the Fitting Fulfillment View and the Fundamentality Theory offer plausible prima facie accounts of a meaningful life. No doubt, there are powerful objections one can level at them.[22] But for our purposes, I think they are useful even if it turns out that they fail as full analyses of meaning. The reason for this is that each of these theories identifies a sufficient condition on living a meaningful life. Moreover, the sufficient conditions they offer are ones in virtue of which the majority of actual meaningful lives count as such. That is, what I'm suggesting is that insofar you are living a meaningful life, it's almost certainly because you satisfy either Wolf's or Metz's condition of meaningfulness. However, what I want to argue below is that a meaningful life according to either of these theories paradigmatically involves and perhaps even requires a pattern of diverse concern. This means that if you're living a meaningful life, it's almost certainly the case that you have a pattern of diverse concerns, commitments, or values. Of course, it's precisely the fact that we care about a pattern of diverse ends and activities that leads us into ambivalence-meriting practical conflicts. After all, if Erica didn't care at all about her parents' welfare, for example, then she would in no way be conflicted about whether to pursue her ambitions or stay in her hometown. It is, in other words, only because she cares about her folks, and that she identifies with that concern that the conflict even arises for her. It seems, then, that living a meaningful life is so paradigmatically connected to patterns of *diverse* concern that it almost certainly requires of us that we regularly face ambivalence-meriting practical conflicts.

---

[22] Nomy Arpaly (2010) and Robert Adams (2010) offer strong responses to Wolf's view. Similarly, Stewart Goetz (2014) has offered important objections to Metz.

## 8.3.2. Meaning and Diversity

Now you might be worried here that nothing about Wolf's or Metz's views requires that paradigm cases of agents leading meaningful lives—agents like Robinson or Munro or Mandela—must be open to ambivalence. In Wolf's case, this worry is to some degree well founded. As Wolf develops her view—if not in spirit, at least in principle—it is consistent with the Fitting Fulfillment View that one's life is wholly dominated by a single concern/activity. But the fact that it might be possible to live a meaningful life even if you only care about one thing that has some positive value doesn't undermine the fact that typically, the meaningfulness of our lives is instantiated by a pattern of diverse concerns. Moreover, it is seems dubious that on Wolf's view, for example, a writer on a par with Robinson or Munro who eschewed all other sources of value in her life would live just as meaningful a life as one who supplemented creative work with other valuable concerns and activities.[23]

This is true for Metz's Fundamentality Theory as well. Recall that that theory stipulates that the meaningfulness of a person's life increases to the degree that that person uses her rational capacities to promote and honor the fundamental conditions of individual and collective existence. So while it might be sufficient on Metz's view that a person's life is meaningful in virtue of single-minded focus on one fundamental concern, the meaningfulness of that person's life is *enhanced* by wider engagement with fundamental human concerns. Because Metz's view explicitly has this scalar feature, it also clearly implicates the value of having a pattern of diverse concerns. After all, most of us, even if we are not concerned to maximize the meaningfulness of our lives, do care about having more meaningful lives when possible. It seems, then, that on both

---

[23] It is also doubtful, though perhaps not entirely germane to this argument, that a person could be such a good writer if she did not have a pattern of thoroughly diverse concerns.

Wolf's and Metz's views, patterns of diverse concern are typically implicated in the realization of meaning in an individual's life and in the degree to which her life is meaningful.

Unfortunately, this alone won't upset the view that unificationists might insist on. Consider that if wholeheartedness is the key to well-functioning agency, then you might think that it's therefore good to be wholeheartedly committed to the sources of meaning in your life. But if you are genuinely wholehearted with respect to some motive, then you must be prepared to either deprioritize or extrude as outlaw any motive that comes into conflict with it. Yet if you relegate a competing motive to a lower status, then it seems that you do not wholeheartedly stand behind that motive any more. And if you extrude some motive entirely from your practical self, then you no longer stand behind it in any sense. In either case, however, you cannot both be wholehearted *and* have a pattern of diverse concerns that often lead to conflicts. Wholeheartedness therefore seems to require a very careful commitment to only care about things that can never come into conflict or to only care about one thing, fully sublimating all other interests to it. The first of these options is difficult to guarantee—how could Agamemnon have possibly known that being a good king could ever be so thoroughly opposed to being a good father? This only leaves open the second option, which explains why unificationists have been inclined to say things like "purity of heart is to will *one* thing" (Kierkegaard 2008; emphasis added).[24]

---

[24] This transition from wholeheartedness to single-mindedness is one Harry Frankfurt strenuously objects to. Specifically he claims that "people do not achieve purity of heart by becoming narrowly focused. The pure heart is the heart of someone who is volitionally unified, and who is thus fully in tact" (2004, 96). The forcefulness of Frankfurt's claims here notwithstanding, he offers no argument for what he says here. Moreover, as I've already argued, it's hard to see how one can be volitionally unified in the sense at stake without unduly narrow focus of concerns or without the exceptional luck of never finding oneself in circumstances in which the elements of your will come into conflict. But getting lucky in this way, if this is indeed a form of luck, is not something under our control; we are passive with respect to it. As a result, getting lucky in this way should not matter for whether we are functioning well as agents.

It is, however, very difficult to square the circle of living a meaningful and single-minded life. Perhaps John Brown, whose devotion to destroying the institution of slavery is sometimes characterized as single-minded, did so. And although he almost certainly was not in fact single-minded—we know, for example, he was a devout man who cared deeply for his family—his life would have been quite meaningful even without those concerns. Yet most of us are not John Browns. Nor are we Nelson Mandelas or Harriet Tubmans or Dietrich Bonhoeffers either—people who made, or at least attempted to make, such great contributions to humankind that their lives would be meaningful even if they lacked a pattern of diverse concerns. Indeed, nothing that most of us identify with is sufficient in itself to make our lives meaningful to this degree. If our lives are meaningful, as I suspect they are for many of us, they are meaningful in a more "unhistoric" way.[25] That is, for most of us, the meaningfulness of our lives is due not to world-altering success issuing from single-minded focus but to the diffusive commitments we all tend to have toward developing ourselves and caring for and living with others. To help flesh out this point, I want to more carefully explain why I am suspicious of single-mindedness.

---

[25] Consider here the concluding passage from George Eliot's *Middlemarch*.

> [Dorothea's] finely touched spirit had still its fine issues, though they were not widely visible. Her full nature, like that river of which Alexander broke the strength, spent itself in channels which had no great name on the earth. But the effect of her being on those around her was incalculably diffusive: for the growing good of the world is partly dependent on unhistoric acts; and that things are not so ill with you and me as they might have been, is half owing to the number who lived faithfully a hidden life, and rest in unvisited tombs. (Eliot 2003)

This statement about what makes Dorothea's life a meaningful one is striking. That she was a "finely touched spirit" living in Victorian England meant that Dorothea's life could not be meaningful for world-historic reasons. But it's hard to read the concluding passages of the novel without thinking that the modest and utterly unhistoric life that Dorothea does lead is no less meaningful for it. Furthermore, it's important to note here that it's very doubtful that those of us who live unhistoric lives should feel bad about a life that might only be meaningful in the way Dorothea's is. Like Dorothea, we should be immensely satisfied with that fate.

In earlier work, Susan Wolf (1982) develops the first step of an argument that single-mindedness is opposed to meaning. She does this by offering an explanation for why this would be so in the case of a life utterly dominated by moral concern. Such a life—the life of a moral saint—she claims, is not an attractive one because it precludes other loves, other activities, and other achievements for their own sake. So, for example, if I am solely focused on maximizing happiness or doing my Kantian duty or whatever impartial morality *de re* requires, then I cannot regard time spent with you in the way that two friends might spend time together as time well spent, since I could have been doing more good were I to have done something else. But this just means that I cannot interact with you in the ways that both cause us to become friends and later constitute to a significant degree what it means for us to remain friends. And even if I can manage to find and enjoy some time with you, if I am really a moral saint, then I will always be *prepared* to get up and leave at the drop of a hat whenever *any* more important moral good might be preserved.[26]

Though Wolf frames this critique of domineering, rationalist conceptions of morality, it also serves as a powerful critique of single-minded commitment to any particular end whatsoever. After all, if single-minded commitment to a single, dominant end is *ever* going to be attractive, rationally defensible, and part of a meaningful life, then surely it will be in the case of single-minded commitment to morality. But it's not. (Indeed, it's not for nothing that in the wake of criticisms like those due to Wolf that defenses of morality began to be more sensitive to the role partiality might have to play within a moral system.)[27]

[26] What Wolf does here is, in essence, to demonstrate why wholehearted commitment to some end (in this case, morality) is inevitably single-minded. If you are wholehearted with respect to some motive, then you will inevitably prioritize it to the detriment or diminishment of all other concerns.

[27] See, for example Nagel 1991, Scheffler 1992, and Keller 2013.

Yet if single-minded concern for and devotion to morality undercuts the meaningfulness of one's life (or, at least, undermines one's ability to pursue other genuinely meaningful ends like friendship or romantic relationships), then surely other, more idiosyncratic ends should not be the singular objects of our concern. That is, if morality isn't something that I should singularly devote myself to, then surely my career, or my aspirations of writing a novel, or my golf game, or my . . . are not things that are *worthy* of such devotion.

Naturally, it's possible that the problem here isn't single-minded devotion per se but is instead *my* single-minded devotion. *I* am not, I confess, uniquely gifted in any particular domain. I suppose I'm fine enough as a philosopher (or at least: I can pull off a passable impression of a fine enough philosopher). But I'm no writer. I don't even have an unfinished novel stuffed away in a (digital) drawer somewhere—just some pipe dreams about writing something more "significant" than the stuff I send out to journals. And, well, the less said about my golf game the better. Perhaps if I were Wittgenstein or George Eliot or Arnold Palmer, then single-mindedness on my part could be major contributor to the meaningfulness of my life. Or at least, one might think that single-mindedness wouldn't obviously cut against the meaningfulness of my life if I too were a "genius" in any of these domains of excellence.

But even this is dubious. Is it really credible that any of these lives would be made *more* meaningful by forgoing relationships with family, friendships with peers, and attempts at stable, honest love relationships in order to become marginally better at philosophy, writing, or golf? I doubt it. And the same is true for any other "genius" that excels in exactly one specific domain. So even if genuine greatness in a domain of the sort we romanticize as requiring single-minded commitment is sufficient for some measure of meaningfulness, it is also a limiting factor, since the presence of other good things would also contribute significantly to the overall meaningfulness of the life.[28]

What's important for a meaningful life, it seems, it not just that one is actively or rationally engaged in some *activity* that has value or is a fundamental condition of human existence, but that one's engagement with objects of value is well distributed. The reason for this should not be surprising at this point. It is, in fact, a completely familiar point: human agents have a wide variety of capacities— cognitive, conative, relational, creative, etc.—and their lives will be most meaningful when they successfully engage and develop the capacities in each of these domains. I care about philosophical endeavors, but I also love my relationships with family and friends, and I also value being a supportive teacher, and I strive to be a re- liable mentor, and it even matters to me that I can (sometimes) tell funny jokes and (occasionally) have a putt for birdie and, when my family is hungry, cook a really satisfying meal. And even if saint- hood is too much, I also still care deeply about being morally good.

Insofar as each of these things contributes to the overall mean- ingfulness of my life, they also often provide me with reasons that are not mutually consistent. That is, the very things I care about the most, the ones that give my life meaning, are also the source of sig- nificant practical conflict. Like Erica in the example I opened the book with, the things I care about often put me at odds with myself with no easy resolution. But if I value myself, if I care about living authentically with integrity, then I won't lament this fact. I will simply be ambivalent when the circumstances call for it.

## 8.4.  Conclusion

If normative competence only *rarely* requires that we be am- bivalent, then although unificationism is false, a practically

---

[28] For more on this point, see Hurka 1987 and Amy Berg (n.d.).

indistinguishable thesis might still be true. What I've tried to argue in this chapter is that normative competence will regularly require us to be ambivalent. It does so because we care about being moral and we care about living meaningful lives. And the conditions for realizing these ends regularly result in very deep practical conflicts. In other words, ambivalence-meriting conflicts are ubiquitous.

This is a heavy blow for unificationism. After all, if unificationism's conception of well-functioning agency is at odds with being a moral person who is living a meaningful life, then so much the worse for unificationism. Why should we care about structuring our wills in a particular way—as unified or wholeheartedly—if that already puts us in opposition to morality and meaning? From this perspective, then, unity and wholeheartedness seem less like forms of freedom than like an alien standard that does nothing to improve or ennoble our lives. We should therefore reject unificationism.

# 9

# Conclusion

## Being Large, Containing Multitudes

In the penultimate section of his "Song of Myself," Walt Whitman (1855) famously asks if he contradicts himself and answers, simply, that he does. To this he adds parenthetically, "I am large, I contain multitudes." This poem—these three short lines in particular—is one of the most famous in American verse. And one reason that it has resonated so strongly is surely the fact that Whitman lays bare a truth that so many genuinely great philosophers seem quite keen to ignore: our selves and, as a result, who we are as agents are fragmented.[1] Each of us cares about, values, and loves so many distinct things, experiences, pursuits, and people that our identities cannot be easily reduced. This, of course, does not mean that we should give no heed to how these elements of our selves come into conflict. But it does mean that the ideal of human agents as unified, perfectly consistent little wholes is itself misguided. It's not just an unachievable ideal; it's also unattractive.

Here we get to the real heart of my disagreement with unificationists. The unificationists claim that autonomous, self-governed action is not possible for ambivalent agents. So too, they worry that a meaningful life—one that a person can affirm and take satisfaction in—is also precluded by ambivalence. And finally, they doubt that the ambivalent agent can live a life of integrity. But if Whitman is right, if we contradict ourselves, if we

---

[1] It seems that "a foolish consistency" is adored, as Emerson claimed, not only by "little . . . philosophers," but also by the greats as well.

*In Praise of Ambivalence*. D. Justin Coates, Oxford University Press. © Oxford University Press 2023.
DOI: 10.1093/oso/9780197652398.003.0009

are large and contain multitudes, then all these worries are not only *not* well founded, they get things exactly backward. In other words, if Whitman is right about what kinds of agents we are, then it will follow that autonomy, meaning, and integrity can each require us to be ambivalent. After all, if my self is large, then how can I be *self*-governed if I simply ignore the authority of major elements of my self? And if I contain multitudes, how can I find meaning by wholly extruding or ignoring some important subset of those constituent elements? And last, if I contradict myself, then in what sense to I exhibit integrity if I do not act and live in a way that reflects the fact that my psychology is fragmented? Autonomy, meaning, and integrity are not the purview of unified, wholehearted agents, at least not if human psychology looks at all like Whitman has proposed.

Naturally, if romanticizing wholeheartedness leads us astray, then so too, we can be led astray by placing too much emphasis on ambivalence. Ambivalence is called for in the face of a difficult practical conflict of a certain sort. Yet, in other cases, exercising our normative competence might entail that we be wholehearted. This might suggest that in some sense the ultimate conclusion of this book is relatively weak. But accepting that suggestion would be a mistake. To be a well-functioning agent, you have to exercise your normative competence, and that will probably mean that sometimes (though not always) you'll need to be ambivalent. As a prospective guide, this is deeply unsatisfying. It may be true that in order to be well-functioning agents we must structure our wills in a way that reflects what reasons (including countervolitional reasons) we have. But without a definitive principle like *be wholehearted* to structure our wills, our grasp on what well-functioning agency requires of us is no better than our grasp on what reasons we have. And this is undoubtedly frustrating. Yet these frustrations must be understood in relation to the fact that they arise only because we are a very special class of agents. It's only because we are normatively competent agents, who, if only imperfectly, are sensitive, attuned, and responsive to normatively significant considerations, that difficultly of structuring our wills arises.

In this respect, ambivalence and the host of frustrations, anxieties, and indignities that often accompany it can be very much like the sense of absurdity that we sometimes feel when living our lives. That feeling, Thomas Nagel (1971) tells us, arises because we are agents who are capable of viewing our own commitments as if from the outside. We thus feel that the seriousness that we take toward those commitments is absurd because we are reflexively aware of the contingencies of those commitments. But though the feeling that our lives are absurd in this sense is at least to some degree unsettling, we can take satisfaction in the fact that the absurdity only comes about because we are agents who possess the capacity to "step back" from our immediate feelings, desires, and ends and evaluate them from a wider, more comprehensive perspective. In other words, we are prone to feel as if our lives are absurd only because we are rational agents.

Similarly, it's only because we are rational agents capable of exercising our normative competence that we are capable of experiencing ambivalence. In other words, the anxiety and stress that we often feel in moments of ambivalence is, at worst, a consequence of the fact that we are rational agents who find ourselves invested in a wide variety of valuable ends. And that's a genuine comfort because it speaks to our capacity for recognizing and responding to worthy goods. Of course, knowing this won't make the decision at hand any easier, but it will allow us to rest assured that we're not making a mistake simply in being ambivalent.

# Works Cited

Adams, Robert M. 2010. "Comment." *Meaning in Life and Why It Matters.* Princeton, NJ: Princeton University Press, 75–84.

Aeschylus. 1984. *The Oresteia.* Trans. Robert Fagles. New York: Penguin Classics.

Alcott, Louisa May. 2007. *Little Women.* New York: Bantam Dell.

Annas, Julia. 1981. *An Introduction to Plato's Republic.* Oxford: Oxford University Press.

Anscombe, G. E. M. 1958. "Modern Moral Philosophy." *Philosophy* 33: 1–19.

Anzaldúa, Gloria. 1987. *Borderlands / La Frontera.* San Francisco: Aunt Lute Books.

Aristotle. 2004. *The Nicomachean Ethics.* Trans. J. A. K. Thomson. New York: Penguin Books.

Arpaly, Nomy. 2003. *Unprincipled Virtue.* New York: Oxford University Press.

Arpaly, Nomy. 2010. "Comment." *Meaning in Life and Why It Matters.* Princeton, NJ: Princeton University Press, 85–91.

Augustine. 1992. *Confessions.* Trans. Henry Chadwick. Oxford: Oxford University Press.

Barvosa, Edwina. 2007. "Mestiza Autonomy as Relational Autonomy: Ambivalence and the Social Character of Free Will." *Journal of Political Philosophy* 15.1: 1–21.

Barvosa, Edwina. 2008. *Wealth of Selves: Multiple Identities, Mestiza Consciousness, and the Subject of Politics.* College Station: Texas A&M Press.

Bentham, Jeremy. 1907. *An Introduction to the Principles of Morals and Legislation.* Oxford: Clarendon Press.

Berg, Amy. n.d. "How and Why to Be Well-Rounded."

Blumenthal-Barby, J. S. 2021. "Ambivalence-Autonomy Compatibilism." *The Philosophy and Psychology of Ambivalence.* Ed. Berit Brogaard and Dimitria Electra Gatzia. New York: Routledge, 49–65.

Bratman, Michael. 1984. "Two Faces of Intention." *Philosophical Review* 93.3: 375–405.

Broad, C. D. 1930. *Five Types of Ethical Theory.* London: Kegan Paul.

Calhoun, Cheshire. 1995. "Standing for Something." *Journal of Philosophy* 92.5: 235–60.

Callard, Agnes. 2018. *Aspiration: The Agency of Becoming.* Oxford: Oxford University Press.

Chang, Ruth. 2015. "Value Pluralism." *International Encyclopedia of the Social & Behavioral Sciences*. 2nd ed. Vol. 25. Ed. James D. Wright. Oxford: Elsevier, 21–26.

Chang, Ruth. 2017. "Hard Choices." *Journal of the American Philosophical Association* 3.1: 1–21.

Clark, Maudemarie. 1990. *Nietzsche on Truth and Philosophy*. Cambridge: Cambridge University Press.

Clark, Maudemarie, and David Dudrick. 2007. "Nietzsche and Moral Objectivity: The Development of Nietzsche's Metaethics." *Nietzsche and Morality*. Ed. Brian Leiter and Neil Sinhababu. Oxford: Oxford University Press, 192–226.

Clark, Maudemarie, and David Dudrick. 2012. *The Soul of Nietzsche's "Beyond Good and Evil"*. Cambridge: Cambridge University Press.

Coates, D. Justin. 2017. "A Wholehearted Defense of Ambivalence." *Journal of Ethics* 21: 419–44.

Conee, Earl. 1982. "Against Moral Dilemmas." *Philosophical Review* 91.1: 87–97.

Cooper, John. 1999. *Reason and Emotion: Essays on Ancient Moral Psychology and Ethical Theory*. Princeton, NJ: Princeton University Press.

Dancy, Jonathan. 2004. *Ethics without Principles*. Oxford: Oxford University Press.

Descartes, René. 1996. *Meditations on First Philosophy*. Trans. John Cottingham. Cambridge: Cambridge University Press.

Dillard, Annie. 2007. *The Maytrees*. New York: HarperCollins.

Eliot, George. 2003. *Middlemarch*. New York: Penguin Classics.

Emerson, Ralph Waldo. 1841/2000. "Self-Reliance." *The Essential Writings of Ralph Waldo Emerson*. Ed. Brooks Atkinson. New York: Random House, 132–53.

Engstrom, Stephen. 2009. *The Form of Practical Knowledge: A Study of the Categorical Imperative*. Cambridge, MA: Harvard University Press.

Feldman, Simon D. and Allan Hazlett. 2021. "Fitting Inconsistency and Reasonable Irresolution," *The Philosophy and Psychology of Ambivalence*. Ed. Berit Brogaard and Dimitria Electra Gatzia. New York: Routledge, 131–46.

Fischer, John Martin. 1994. *The Metaphysics of Free Will*. Oxford: Blackwell Publishers.

Fischer, John Martin, and Mark Ravizza. 1998. *Responsibility and Control*. Cambridge: Cambridge University Press.

Foot, Philippa. 2001. *Natural Goodness*. Oxford: Oxford University Press.

Frankfurt, Harry. 1971. "Freedom of the Will and the Concept of a Person." *Journal of Philosophy* 68: 5–20.

Frankfurt, Harry. 1982. "The Importance of What We Care About." *Synthese* 53.2: 257–72.

Frankfurt, Harry. 1988. "Identification and Wholeheartedness." *The Importance of What We Care About*. Cambridge: Cambridge University Press, 159–76.

Frankfurt, Harry. 1992. "The Faintest Passion." *Proceedings and Addresses of the American Philosophical Association* 66.3: 5–16.

Frankfurt, Harry. 1999. "Autonomy, Necessity, and Love." *Autonomy, Volition, and Love*. Cambridge: Cambridge University Press, 129–41.

Frankfurt, Harry. 2004. *The Reasons of Love*. Princeton, NJ: Princeton University Press.

Gemes, Ken. 2009. "Nietzsche on Free Will, Autonomy, and the Sovereign Individual." *Nietzsche on Freedom and Autonomy*. Ed. Ken Gemes and Simon May. Oxford: Oxford University Press, 33–50.

Goetz, Stewart. 2014. Review of *Meaning in Life*. *Notre Dame Philosophical Reviews*. June 22, 2014.

Goldman, Alan. 2009. *Reasons from Within: Desires and Values*. Oxford: Oxford University Press.

Greenspan, Patricia. 1995. *Practical Guilt: Moral Dilemmas, Emotions, and Social Norms*. Oxford: Oxford University Press.

Gunnarsson, Logi. 2014. "In Defense of Ambivalence and Alienation." *Ethical Theory and Moral Practice* 17.1: 13–26.

Harris, Kenneth Marc. 1988. *Hypocrisy and Self-Deception in Hawthorne's Fiction*. Charlottesville: University of Virginia Press.

Hawthorne, Nathaniel. 2007. *The Scarlet Letter*. New York: Oxford University Press.

Herman, Barbara. 1993. *The Practice of Moral Judgment*. Cambridge, MA: Harvard University Press.

Hill, Thomas E. 1971. "Kant on Imperfect Duty and Supererogation." *Kant Studien* 62: 55–76.

Hume, David. 2000. *A Treatise of Human Nature*. Ed. David Fate Norton and Mary J. Norton. Oxford: Oxford University Press.

Hurka, Thomas. 1987. "The Well-Rounded Life." *Journal of Philosophy* 84.12: 727–46.

Hurka, Thomas. 1993. *Perfectionism*. New York: Oxford University Press.

Hussain, Nadeem. 2007. "Honest Illusion: Valuing for Nietzsche's Free Spirits." *Nietzsche and Morality*. Ed. Brian Leiter and Neil Sinhababu. Oxford: Oxford University Press, 157–91.

Irwin, Terence. 1995. *Plato's Ethics*. Oxford: Oxford University Press.

Jaworska, Agnieszka. 2007. "Caring and Internality." *Philosophy and Phenomenological Research* 74.3: 529–68.

Jech, Alexander. 2013. "To Will One Thing." *American Philosophical Quarterly* 50.2: 153–66.

Kant, Immanuel. 1998. *Groundwork of the Metaphysics of Morals*. Trans. Mary Gregor. Cambridge: Cambridge University Press.

Katsafanas, Paul. 2016. *The Nietzschean Self: Moral Psychology, Agency, and the Unconscious*. Oxford: Oxford University Press.

Keller, Simon. 2013. *Partiality*. Princeton, NJ: Princeton University Press.

Kierkegaard, Sören. 2008. *Purity of the Heart Is to Will One Thing*. Floyd, VA: Wilder Publications.

Kirwin, Claire. 2017. "Pulling Oneself Up by the Hair: Understanding Nietzsche on the Freedom of the Will." *Inquiry* 61: 82–99.

Korsgaard, Christine M. 1986. "Kant's Formula of Humanity." *Kant Studien* 77: 183–202.

Korsgaard, Christine M. 1996. *The Sources of Normativity*. Cambridge: Cambridge University Press.

Korsgaard, Christine M. 1999. "Self-Constitution in the Ethics of Plato and Kant." *Journal of Ethics* 3: 1–29.

Korsgaard, Christine M. 2009. *Self-Constitution: Agency, Identity, and Integrity*. New York: Oxford University Press.

Lear, Gabriel. 2005. *Happy Lives and the Highest Good: An Essay on Aristotle Nicomachean Ethics*. Princeton, NJ: Princeton University Press.

Leiter, Brian. 2007. "Nietzsche's Theory of the Will." *Philosophers' Imprint* 7: 1–15.

Leiter, Brian. 2015. *Nietzsche on Morality*. New York: Routledge.

Lincoln, Abraham. 1858. "The House Divided." Delivered June 16.

Magnus, Bernd. 1978. *Nietzsche's Existential Imperative*. Bloomington: Indiana University Press.

Maguire, Barry. 2017. "There Are No Reasons for Affective Attitudes." *Mind* 127.507: 779–805.

McDowell, John. 1979. "Virtue and Reason." *The Monist* 62.3: 331–50.

Metz, Thaddeus. 2013. *Meaning in Life: An Analytic Study*. Oxford: Oxford University Press.

Mill, J. S. 1998. *Utilitarianism*. Ed. Roger Crisp. Oxford: Oxford University Press.

Moore, G. E. 1903. *Principia Ethica*. Cambridge: Cambridge University Press.

Nagel, Thomas. 1971. "The Absurd." *Journal of Philosophy* 68.20: 716–27.

Nagel, Thomas. 1979. "The Fragmentation of Value." *Mortal Questions*. Cambridge: Cambridge University Press, 128–41.

Nagel, Thomas. 1991. *Equality and Partiality*. New York: Oxford University Press.

Nehamas, Alexander. 1980. "The Eternal Recurrence." *Philosophical Review* 89.3: 331–56.

Nietzsche, Friedrich. 1995. *Thus Spoke Zarathustra: A Book for All and None*. Trans. Walter Kaufmann. New York: Modern Library.

Nietzsche, Friedrich. 2001. *The Gay Science*. Trans. Josephine Nauckhoff. Cambridge: Cambridge University Press.

Nietzsche, Friedrich. 2003. *Beyond Good and Evil*. Trans. R. J. Hollingdale. New York: Penguin Classics.

Nussbaum, Martha. 2001. *The Fragility of Goodness: Luck and Ethics in Greek Tragedy and Philosophy*. Rev. ed. Cambridge: Cambridge University Press.

O'Connor, Flannery. 1971. "Good Country People." *The Complete Stories*. New York: Farrar, Straus and Giroux.

Parfit, Derek. 2011. *On What Matters*. Oxford: Oxford University Press.

Paul, L. 2014. A. *Transformative Experience*. New York: Oxford University Press.

Plato. 2004. *Republic*. Trans. C. D. C. Reeve. Indianapolis: Hackett.

Poltera, Jacqui. 2011. "Is Ambivalence an Agential Vice?" *Philosophical Explorations* 13.3: 293–305.

Railton, Peter. 1984. "Alienation, Consequentialism, and the Demands of Morality." *Philosophy and Public Affairs* 13: 134–71.

Razinsky, Hili. 2017. *Ambivalence: A Philosophical Exploration*. London: Rowman & Littlefield.

Ridley, Aaron. 1997. "Nietzsche's Greatest Weight." *Journal of Nietzsche Studies* 14: 19–25.

Robinson, Marilynne. 2004. *Gilead*. New York: Picador.

Ross, W. D. 1930. *The Right and the Good*. Oxford: Oxford University Press.

Scanlon. T. M. 1998. *What We Owe to Each Other*. Cambridge, MA: Harvard University Press.

Scheffler, Samuel. 1992. *Human Morality*. Oxford: Oxford University Press.

Scheffler, Samuel. 2011. "Valuing." *Reasons and Recognition: Essays on the Philosophy of T.M. Scanlon*. Ed. R. J. Wallace, R. Kumar, and S. Freeman. Oxford: Oxford University Press, 23–42.

Schroeder, Mark. 2007. *Slaves of the Passions*. New York: Oxford University Press.

Schroeder, Timothy, and Nomy Arpaly. 1999. "Alienation and Externality." *Canadian Journal of Philosophy* 29.3: 371–87.

Shafer-Landau, Russ. 2003. *Moral Realism: A Defence*. Oxford: Oxford University Press.

Shoemaker, David. 2003. "Caring, Identification, and Agency." *Ethics* 114: 88–118.

Sidgwick, Henry. 1874. *The Methods of Ethics*. London: Macmillan.

Silk, Alex. 2015. "Nietzschean Constructivism: Ethics and Metaethics for All and None." Special issue: "Nietzsche's Moral Psychology." *Inquiry* 58.3: 244–80.

Smart, J. J. C. 1973. "An Outline of a System of Utilitarian Ethics." *Utilitarianism: For and Against*. New York: Cambridge University Press, 3–76.

Soll, Ivan. 1973. "Reflections on Recurrence." *Nietzsche: A Collection of Critical Essays*. Ed. Robert Solomon. Garden City, NY: Doubleday.

Sommers, Tamler. 2018. *Why Honor Matters*. New York: Basic Books.

Spinoza, Baruch. 2000. *Ethics*. Trans. G. H. R. Parkinson. Oxford: Oxford Philosophical Texts.

Strawson, P. F. 1961. "Social Morality and the Individual Ideal." *Philosophy* 36.136: 1–17.

Swindell, J. S. 2010. "Ambivalence." *Philosophical Explorations* 13.1: 23–34.

Velleman, J. David. 1992. "What Happens When Someone Acts?" *Mind* 101.403: 461–81.

Velleman, J. David. 2002. "Identification and Identity." *The Contours of Agency: Essays on Themes from Harry Frankfurt*. Ed. Sarah Buss and Lee Overton. Cambridge, MA: MIT Press, 91–123.

Wallace, R. Jay. 1994. *Responsibility and the Moral Sentiments*. Cambridge, MA: Harvard University Press.

Watson, Gary. 1975. "Free Agency." *Journal of Philosophy* 72: 205–20.

Watson, Gary. 1987. "Free Action and Free Will." *Mind* 96: 154–72.

Watson, Gary. 1990. "On the Primacy of Character." *Identity, Character, and Morality*. Ed. Owen Flanagan and Amelie Rorty. Cambridge, MA: MIT Press, 449–70.

Watson, Gary. 1996. "Two Faces of Responsibility." *Philosophical Topics* 24.2: 227–48.

Whitman, Walt. [1855] 1892. *Leaves of Grass*.

Williams, Bernard. 1965. "Ethical Consistency." *Proceedings of the Aristotelian Society* 39: 103–24.

Williams, Bernard. 1979. "Internal and External Reasons." *Rational Action*. Ed. Ross Harrison. Cambridge: Cambridge University Press, 101–13.

Williams, Bernard. 1981. "Moral Luck." *Moral Luck: Philosophical Papers, 1973–1980*. Cambridge: Cambridge University Press, 20–39.

Williams, Bernard. 1985. *Ethics and the Limits of Philosophy*. London: Fontana.

Williams, Bernard. 1993. *Shame and Necessity*. Berkeley: University of California Press.

Wolf, Susan. 1982. "Moral Saints." *Journal of Philosophy* 79.8: 419–39.

Wolf, Susan. 2001. "The Moral of Moral Luck." *Philosophic Exchange* 31.1: 5–19.

Wolf, Susan. 2002. "The True, the Good, and the Loveable: Frankfurt's Avoidance of Objectivity." *Contours of Agency: Essays on Themes from Harry Frankfurt*. Ed. Sarah Buss and Lee Overton. Cambridge, MA: MIT Press, 227–44.

Wolf, Susan. 2010. *Meaning in Life and Why It Matters*. Princeton, NJ: Princeton University Press.

Wolf, Susan. 2015. "The Meaning of Lives." *The Variety of Values: Essays on Morality, Meaning, & Love*. New York: Oxford University Press, 89–106.

# Index